How to Buy
the
Best Sailboat

HOW TO BUY
THE
BEST
SAILBOAT

AN UPDATED EDITION OF THE
LEADING CONSUMER GUIDE
WITH A NEW CHAPTER ON
SELLING A BOAT

CHUCK GUSTAFSON

HEARST MARINE BOOKS
NEW YORK

Library of Congress Cataloging-in-Publication Data

Gustafson, Charles.
    How to buy the best sailboat / by Charles Gustafson.—An updated edition of the leading consumer guide with a new chapter on selling a boat.
        p.   cm.
    ISBN 0-688-10987-X
    1. Sailboats. 2. Sailboats—Equipment and supplies.   I. Title.
GV811.4.G85   1991
623.8'223'029—dc20   91-18273
                                                                                        CIP

Printed in the United States of America

3   4   5   6   7   8   9   10

BOOK DESIGN BY PATRICE FODERO

*This book is dedicated to Alice—
co-skipper, friend, wife, and personal
editor.
She has kept me off the rocks more than
once.*

ACKNOWLEDGMENTS

I would like to thank all those who have supported and helped with this new edition. Alice, our boat's best helmsperson, who tries to keep me from procrastinating and gave me much needed help with mine grammar, my speeellllinng, and my punc?tu!!!ati..on. Barbara Henderson, who took most of the photos used in this book without falling off one dock. Betty Hames, who snuck her dog, Holly, into many of her excellent drawings. Connie Roosevelt, my editor at Hearst, who had the idea for this new edition and got it approved. Julie Morgan, who valiantly tried to retrieve my book revisions from a computer disk after I brilliantly deleted both my working and backup copies. My students, who continually ask the hard questions that help keep me current. My clients, who have provided me with so many examples of what should and **should not** be replicated. My Mountaineer sailing friends, from whom I have learned so much and who have been patient with my exhaustive replies to what they thought were simple questions. And finally Mousse, our dog with the water/swimming obsession, who played hooky with me when I should have been writing.

CONTENTS

14 • *Contents*

INTRODUCTION

TEN RULES OF SAILBOAT OWNERSHIP

These rules apply to all sailors as soon as they start considering buying their own boat. They become inapplicable when sailing is given up for gardening, bridge, finger painting, or similar activities.

Rule 1: Your current sailboat is too small.

Rule 2: Your current sailboat is too large.

Rule 3: It is easier to spend dollars on the boat than on (a) your house, (b) your car, or (c) your children's education.

Rule 4: If you don't use your sailboat, nothing will break (or almost nothing).

Rule 5: Equipment lost overboard is always new, expensive, one of a kind, irreplaceable, or all of the above.

Rule 6: Whenever you are working on the boat there is a great sailing wind. Conversely, whenever the boat is shipshape and ready to go sailing, either (a) the wind has died, or (b) the weather has turned miserable.

Rule 7: The amount of time you spend maintaining your

Rule 1: Your current sailboat is too small

boat increases geometrically in relationship to your boat's displacement and complexity.

Rule 8: The number of people that a sailboat can comfortably daysail is equal to the number of berths claimed by the builder. The number of people that a sailboat can comfortably sleep is the number of berths claimed by the builder divided by three.

Rule 9: Any boat that can outsail your own boat is (a) crewed by professionals, (b) dangerously light and underbuilt, or (c) a hot high-tech expensive racing boat.

Rule 10: Owning a sailboat is a lot like raising a teenager; it is a love-hate relationship.

Rule 5: Equipment lost overboard is always new, expensive, one of a kind, irreplaceable, or all of the above.

ABOUT THIS BOOK

The "Ten Rules of Sailboat Ownership" aren't fiction; they're reality. This guide is intended to prepare you for that reality, starting with the dream, through the tough compromises, the many decisions on design, construction, and equipment, the detailed inspections, pricing, and the final negotiations. The book also covers many of the overlooked details of ownership that follow the actual purchase. The range of topics is wide. Each could only be examined individually through extensive research and lots of sailing. Because the coverage is broad, some topics have received only a cursory review. For those readers who need more detail on construction, outfitting, or repair, I refer you to the many specialized books available. My focus is the purchase of new and used monohull fiberglass boats from twenty to fifty feet in length and of standard design, construction, and equipment. This new edition has a completely revised chapter on performance criteria, a revised bibliography, a new chapter on selling a boat, the latest versions of my sailboat evaluation checklists, and major revisions on blistering, sails, engines, running rigging, anchors, and many other topics.

THE AUTHOR'S BIAS

As you pick up this guide, you will already have your own sailing experiences and opinions on sailboats. I hope I can add to your knowledge base. I have tried to be objective and to include only information that generally is accepted within the sailing community. However, sailors can be an opinionated and stubborn lot (myself excepted, of course), and you would do well to read other sailors' thinking on these same topics.

It will be helpful if you understand what some of my biases are as you start this guide. First, I am cruising oriented. My own experience has been in day sailing and coastal cruising.

Blue-water passages aren't planned for the immediate future, although our boat is very close to being blue-water ready.

Although I favor cruising, like the serious racer I hate to see someone outsail us, whether it is a cruiser, racer-cruiser, or a state-of-the-art racing boat. We have participated in many races in which our opponent didn't know a race was taking place. I also follow the constantly evolving developments in racing design and equipment, since many of the successful innovations eventually are transferred to cruisers and daysailers. The serious racer should thus find much of use in this guide.

Another bias that will be apparent is that I am compulsive about construction quality, outfitting, maintenance, and safety. I would rather sail in a properly designed, equipped, and prepared sailboat of thirty feet than a much larger one of dubious character. This translates into a preference for construction characteristics and equipment that are one or two sizes stronger than would be required under normal conditions. I also prefer simplicity in design and ease of function. My rationale for this is that it is less expensive in both the short and long run, makes modifications and installation of equipment on the boat less difficult, and results in more time sailing and less time spent in maintenance. Remember, Murphy's Law rules a boat. The water-pump impeller never disintegrates at the dock but waits until you are in a narrow channel bucking a five-knot foul current. If you are the type who doesn't believe in life jackets or who intends to buy a boat on Monday and set sail for Hawaii on Friday, you will find my approach frustrating.

Lastly, I have a strong bias for sailboats that sail fast and steer well. Though nothing pleases my eye more than a traditional boat with topsails pulling and jibs set on a twenty-five-foot bowsprit, my interest doesn't go further unless I know that it will sail in less than 10 knots of wind (5 or 2 is even better), that it will surf down a wave crest without pitchpoling or broaching at the smallest inattention to the helm, that it will sail at least 45° to the true wind, and that it can be handled smartly in a crowded anchorage under either sail or power.

ABOUT THE READER

This guide has been written for a broad range of interests. The novice sailor and first-time owner should find it useful because it offers a rational approach to the entire process of buying a sailboat and provides a comprehensive discussion of the majority of criteria that should be considered in making the purchase. If only 10 percent of the criteria are understood and applied, the first-time owner will have made a better decision than most. The other 90 percent of the criteria will become clearer as experience is gained.

For the more experienced sailors moving up to a larger boat, this guide should fill gaps in their knowledge and provide ideas for judging the next boat.

Finally, this guide should be useful to those experienced sailors who are looking for new ideas on modifying, equipping, and outfitting their boats, who desire a discussion of the advantages and disadvantages of various approaches, or who appreciate the availability of ready-made checklists and work sheets.

THE INTENT OF THIS GUIDE

This new edition is intended to help you define your sailing goals and your realistic requirements for a boat. The book provides a comprehensive approach to boat selection, which takes your unique situation into account. Specific criteria that you can use in evaluating potential boats are outlined. The idea is to help you make the "hard buy" at the best possible price. Even if you use only a portion of the suggestions in this guide, you will be able to make a better selection than the average "hull thumper," with fewer postpurchase surprises and regrets.

I.

LEARNING FROM OTHERS' EXPERIENCES

As you get serious about sailing and owning a boat you should start developing a broad knowledge base about boats and seamanship. Keep in mind that sailing involves learning more than just which way the wind blows against the sails. One of the most challenging and yet satisfying aspects of sailing is that it involves many relatively complex areas that can be mastered at every level from amateur to expert. Most of us can spend a lifetime sailing and still not learn everything a sailor should know. The highly skilled sailor is best represented by the shorthanded cruising sailor who must be at least minimally proficient in all the areas necessary to sail and live comfortably and safely. Skills that quickly become necessary include helmsmanship and sail handling in a variety of conditions; engine and mechanical installation, maintenance and repair; woodworking; fiberglass and metal repair; surface refinishing; electronics; plumbing; sewing and sail repair; provisioning, nutrition, and cooking; navigation and weather; first aid; scuba diving; and on and on.

While firsthand experience is invaluable in all of these areas, much can be learned from other people's experiences. It is pointless to reinvent the wheel on most decisions, purchases, and installations if someone else can save you the time, frustration, and dollar costs of the trial and error method. Save that method for those times when you need a totally unique solution or where alternative approaches haven't been developed. Read until you reach your saturation point on every aspect of sailing, sailboats, and seamanship. Read about design, construction methods, various materials used in construction, maintenance, repairs, emergency procedures, boat handling, and cooking afloat. Read about general seamanship and other sailors' experiences sailing and cruising in a variety of places and conditions. From this you will begin to develop an information base for future reference, an appreciation of the powers of Mother Nature, and a realistic understanding of sailing into which you can integrate your own experiences and desires.

MAGAZINES

One of the quickest ways to assimilate a great deal of up-to-date information from a variety of perspectives is to read sailing magazines. The better ones will include anecdotal information about cruises and helpful cruising tips, covering the full gamut of trip planning, preparation, and seamanship. Most of these also have a "how-to-do-it" section, offer tips on sailing technique, and discuss and hopefully evaluate a variety of sailboats and boating equipment. New sailing books are sometimes serialized in a sailing magazine before they are published in book form. Go to your local newsstand or marine bookstore and try several different magazines for a few months. The best initial mix is to subscribe to at least one national and one local or regional sailing magazine.

To help you get started, the following represents some of my favorite national magazines:

Boat Journal. Emphasis is on smaller boats, power and sail.

Cruising World. Excellent substantive articles. Focus obviously is cruising.

Motor Boating & Sailing. Good technical how-to section.

Practical Sailor. Consumer oriented. Evaluates boats and equipment. Newsletter format twice a month. More expensive because no ads.

Sail. Partial racing orientation. Good sailing technique articles.

Sailing. Large format. Superb photography. Lots of boat reviews. Excellent column by Bob Perry reviewing new designs.

Soundings. Newspaper format. Regional editions.

WoodenBoat. Emphasis obviously is on wood.

BOOKS

The books on design, boat and sail handling, outfitting, maintenance, and other sailing subjects seem to be endless. The following, some of my favorites, may be particularly helpful as you select and outfit a boat.

Chapman, Charles F. *Piloting, Seamanship and Small Boat Handling.* New edition every few years. N.Y.: Hearst Marine Books.

Chappell, Alan. *Sailboat Buyer's Guide.* Long Beach, Miss.: Sea Shore Publications. Listing with specs of 1,019 sailboats.

Coles, K. Adlard. *Heavy Weather Sailing.* Clinton, N.Y.: John De Graff, Inc. Teaches respect for Mother Nature. Essential reading for those at risk of heavy weather, especially offshore.

Cornell, Jimmy. *Ocean Cruising Survey.* Dobbs Ferry, N.Y.: Sheridan House. Good practical information on what boats and equipment cruisers are really using, not what the "experts" tell you to buy.

Cruising Club of America, Technical Committee of. *Desirable and Undesirable Characteristics of Offshore Yachts.* Ed. John Rousmaniere. N.Y.: W. W. Norton & Co. Required reading for anyone contemplating buying a boat for offshore.

Hiscock, Eric. Anything written by this late lifelong sailor. Several of his titles include *Atlantic Cruise; Come Aboard; Cruise in Wanderer III; Cruising Under Sail; Southwest in Wanderer IV; Two Yachts, Two Voyages; Wandering Under Sail.*

Kinney, Francis S. *Skene's Elements of Yacht Design.* New York: Dodd Mead. This is a classic book of yacht design.

Marshall, Roger. *A Sailor's Guide to Production Sailboats.* New York: Hearst Marine Books. A listing with specs of over 400 sailboats.

Nicolson, Ian. *Surveying Small Craft.* Dobbs Ferry, N.Y.: Sheridan House, Inc. Some of the terminology and procedures are different in England, but this is still an excellent overview of the how and what of a survey.

Pardey, Lin and Larry. Lin and Larry espouse the "go small, go cheap, go now" philosophy. Two of their titles include *Cruising in Seraffyn* and *Seraffyn's Mediterranean Adventure.*

Practical Sailor, the Editors of. *The Complete Book of Sailboat Buying, Vols. I & II.* Riverside, CT: Belvoir Publications, Inc. Consumer oriented. Based on material from the magazine. The only other sailboat buying book I can fully endorse. Vol. II includes all the boats reviewed in the magazine up to the book's publication date.

Roth, Hal. Anything by this author is instructive. Two of his better known titles are *After 50,000 Miles* (W. W. Norton, 1977) and *Two Against Cape Horn* (W. W. Norton, 1968).

Rousmaniere, John. *The Annapolis Book of Seamanship.* Very comprehensive and written specifically for sailors. Good companion volume to Chapman's.

Royce, Patrick. *Royce's Sailing Illustrated.* Revised editions published frequently. Excellent reference handbook on sailboats, rigging, and technique.

Sail Magazine. Sailboat & Equipment Directory. Published annually. Good resource for new boats and equipment.

Seven Seas Cruising Association. *Equipment Survey.* 521 S. Andrews Ave., Suite 10, Fort Lauderdale, FL 33301. Excellent information on what works and doesn't work from world cruisers and live-aboards.

Sherwood, Richard M. *A Field Guide to Sailboats.* Boston: Houghton Mifflin Co. A listing with specs on 230 sailboats.

Smith, LeCain, and Moir, Sheila. *Steel Away, A Guidebook to the World of Steel Sailboats.* Port Townsend, Washington: Windrose Productions. Good overview for those interested in steel boats.

Street, Donald. *The Ocean Sailing Yacht, Vols. I and II.* New York: W. W. Norton. Comprehensive and authoritative. Particularly good if you are shopping for an older boat.

Warren, Nigel. *Metal Corrosion in Boats.* Camden, Maine: International Marine. Warren addresses this difficult technical subject so that a lay person can understand it. Excellent reference for all boats, not just for the metal boat buyer/owner.

Expand your sailing expertise by reading, joining a sailing club, crewing on a variety of boats, sifting the opinions of your sailing friends, and/or chartering. It is important to get a wide range of information. Even though many methods, designs, and types of equipment are widely accepted, there are still conflicting views among experienced and respected sailors. YOU have to decide which views mesh with your comfort, risk, budget, pleasure, and frustration level.

What follows is my view of the criteria that are useful in selecting your sailboat. While I generally follow accepted norms, you may desire to subtract from, add to, or modify my criteria.

II.

SAILBOAT SELECTION PREREQUISITES

The single most important step in selecting a sailboat is to delineate clearly your personal and financial constraints, the type of sailing you hope to do immediately and in the future, and your initial expectations of a boat. If you take this first step seriously, you will dramatically increase the probability of a good match between your boat and you. Unfortunately, many potential owners fail to pursue this analysis except on a superficial level. Consequently, they have unsatisfactory ownership experiences. The mismatches vary: a blue-water round-the-world cruiser being sailed or weekended on a lake; an underrigged heavy boat being sailed in a light wind area; a floating condominium being sailed offshore; a boat of questionable construction and design being sailed around the world. Whatever the mismatch, the results are often unfortunate: termination of a live-aboard experiment because of cramped quarters; an aborted cruise because of an unseaworthy boat; too many days spent working on the boat and too few days sailing; more motoring than sailing on a poor performing boat; and at the extreme end, injuries and lost lives.

To increase your odds of avoiding these perils, think about your prerequisites. Be tough and honest with yourself. Ask yourself whether your assumptions are realistic, conservative, or optimistic. Put all of your requirements in writing and then discuss and/or negotiate them with everyone who will be using the boat, involved in its maintenance and financial support, or seriously affected by your involvement.

The following represents a "starter" set of questions and issues from which you can develop your own list of prerequisites for selecting a sailboat.

GENERAL CONSIDERATIONS

What is your experience level in boating, sailing, and mechanical systems? What are your current and potential skills in both sailing and maintenance? What are your athletic inclinations? Would you enjoy hiking out over the waves all day? Who will go forward on a pitching foredeck in 20-knot winds to take down a No. 1 genoa that's been kept up too long?

What are the trade-offs to owning a boat and sailing? Will you feel forced to use the boat because of your investment? Will you tire of eating macaroni and cheese to help pay for it? Will you miss those weekends in the mountains or on the tennis courts?

FINANCIAL CONSTRAINTS

What is the maximum down payment or outright purchase cost you can afford? How much money is available from your take-home income for monthly payments? How stable is your income?

Did you remember to set aside money for equipping your boat? This can run from 20 to 50 percent of the "sail-away" price on a new boat and may be comparable on a used boat that is poorly equipped or requires extensive modifications or repairs. Twenty to 30 percent for outfitting is a good rule of thumb. How desperately will you want that new spinnaker in a year or two? Have you budgeted for those items that seem optional now but may quickly become necessities?

What about insurance? A good marine policy will cost approximately 1 percent of the insured value of your boat per year. What about maintenance, moorage, and unforeseen accidents such as that fouled anchor left behind in Port Blakely or that winch handle knocked overboard on your first sail?

How long before you resell the boat? Will this be a learner boat, your last boat, or a stepping-stone boat? The shorter your planned ownership, the more important local resale value and marketability will be.

HOW WILL YOU USE THE BOAT?

Will the boat be raced, cruised, or chartered? Do you plan to sail in lakes and rivers, coastal or offshore? Are you a dockside, fair- or heavy-weather sailor?

How many days per year will you use the boat, and in which seasons? Will the boat be used primarily for day sailing or overnight cruises? How many nights per year do you expect to sleep on the boat, and in which seasons? What is the length of the maximum cruise you expect to take with this boat? How many people do you expect the boat to comfortably handle on a day sail and on overnight cruises?

How much motoring do you intend or will you have to do? Are you easily frustrated when the wind is light or the tide adverse? Do you typically have commitments on Monday mornings that can't be missed because of fluky winds?

PERSONAL VALUES

How important are the aesthetics of the boat to you? How important is quality of design and construction? Do you enjoy "roughing it" or do you prefer more of the creature comforts?

Do you like a responsive helm? How important is ability to point and boat speed? How many boats can pass you before you reach your frustration level?

Will you enjoy maintaining a boat? Will you maintain it at all? What will you enjoy more—working on the boat or sailing it?

III.

ALTERNATIVE WAYS TO ACCESS A SAILBOAT

Your first decision, once you have decided to start sailing, is how to gain access to a boat. Obviously, most of the readers of this guide will have thought of buying. But is purchasing the right approach for you at this point in your sailing career? There are many sailors who don't own boats and do a great deal of sailing. Perhaps they are novices who are unsure of their level of commitment or feel they are too green to own. They may be individuals who can't commit money to a boat. Or they may be experienced sailors who have the means to own a boat but don't want the responsibility of ownership just yet. I consider my course on "How to Buy the Best Sailboat" successful if several of the students decide NOT to buy. If this is your decision after reading this guide, it doesn't mean that you won't ever own a boat but only that the cold realities of ownership don't fit your circumstances at this time.

The following represent the major ways to go sailing. Each has its own advantages and disadvantages. Pick the one that best meets your current circumstances. After you have reviewed the entire guide, reread this chapter and decide whether your opinion of the best alternative has changed.

CREWING ON OTHER PEOPLE'S BOATS

The easiest way to go sailing is with friends who already own boats. Make your sailing interests known to them, but don't be subtle. Volunteer to help with boat maintenance, indicate your willingness to serve as a committed member of a racing crew, and accept all last-minute sailing invitations. All of these strategies will help get you on a boat. If you don't have any receptive sailing acquaintances, hang out at the docks and inquire about boats that need crew. Put up notices indicating your sailing interests at docks, marine stores, and sailing clubs. Or take out a "personals" ad in a sailing magazine. When you do get an invitation to sail, do your best to ensure that it will be repeated. This means adapting yourself to the boat's routine and the skipper's preferred methods, being alert to help the rest of the crew with their tasks, being honest with the skipper about your capabilities, and being sensitive to your "compatibility factor" with the skipper and the crew.

Crewing on someone else's boat is a very inexpensive way to go sailing. With a talented and experienced skipper and crew, you may have a chance to learn a great deal of sailing technique and seamanship in a quasi-apprenticeship. If you are aggressive, you may also have the opportunity to sail on a variety of boats, perhaps in several different geographic areas.

The difficulty with this alternative is that you are completely dependent upon other skippers and their schedules, plans, and sailing habits. You may also become a specialist on the crew—e.g., in navigation, cooking, or foredeck work—and never have a chance to adequately learn and practice the myriad skills that go into sailing a boat. In some instances, your mentors (skipper or crew) may also be poor instructors or have incompatible personalities.

SAILING CLUBS

Sailing clubs can be located by attending boat shows or checking the Yellow Pages. The advantages of clubs are several. They are relatively low cost, particularly when usage increases beyond the once-a-month sail. They usually offer more than one type and size of boat for sailing, though access to larger boats may be limited. Clubs often include sailing instruction and provide access to sailing partners and crew. Access to boats is usually quite good in the off season, when the wind is at its best, although this period also overlaps with the storm season. Finally, apart from the normal cleanup and unrigging of the boat, maintenance is usually taken care of by the club.

One major disadvantage of sailing clubs, at least in the long term, is that there is little incentive to learn how the boat's equipment works or how to repair and maintain it. These are important skills for the boat owner and serious cruiser, who must be self-reliant. Further, a sailing club's boats are usually very basically rigged and equipped for the average novice sailor. As your level of skill increases, this limitation becomes more and more bothersome. Because of the minimal outfitting and the beating the club boat takes from frequent use, even the best designs will usually perform below optimum levels. It may also be difficult to reserve a boat during the peak sailing season or on those exceptionally good days that occur in the off season.

CHARTERING

Chartering has a number of advantages. The cost of intermittent chartering is usually substantially less than owning a boat of comparable size. For example, the annual cost of boat insurance alone may be more than a one-week charter. For the price of a new spinnaker you may be able to charter one or two weeks. A month of bareboat chartering in the Caribbean might be close to the break-even point of annual ownership costs.

Cost is not the only advantage. Apart from the usual cleanup and minor repairs while under way, outfitting and repairs are usually handled by the charter company. Chartering also provides an opportunity to sail many types and sizes of boats in a variety of cruising areas in this country and overseas. This can provide the prospective boat owner with the chance to trial sail several or more boats under a wide range of conditions. It also permits sailors who love traveling but have a tight time budget to try out many cruising areas without taking a leave of absence or selling their houses. In terms of both dollar and time commitment, chartering allows more flexibility in pursuing alternate leisure activities, for example, skiing heavily one year instead of sailing.

Chartering does have some disadvantages, some of which echo the sailing club experience. There is little incentive to learn how the equipment works or how to repair or maintain it. Again, these soon become necessary skills for the serious sailor. Even if you have the desire, repairs may be difficult or even impossible because of unfamiliarity with the boat's systems or lack of spare parts or tools. If the charter fleet has a "chase boat" and a good maintenance program, this will usually not be a problem. If the charter fleet doesn't provide these services, you may be inconvenienced during your cruise, or worse, have your vacation seriously disrupted.

Another problem with chartering is that the chartered boat is either outfitted and equipped for a specific owner or has been designed and set up for the "average" client. This may be fine for a one-week cruise, but the charter boat will usually not fit your specific needs for long-distance sailing and extended trips.

SHARED OWNERSHIP

With shared ownership, you split the cost and the maintenance responsibilities. This decreases the financial and time commitment required of the individual partners. In addition, shared ownership may provide you with constant fair-weather/foul-weather sailing companions.

The disadvantages of jointly owning a boat can be significant. For example, your sailing time is confined to whatever schedule has been agreed upon. You may disagree with the other co-owners on the basic boat design, equipment, maintenance, or the moorage location. In addition, you may have different sailing preferences, for example, fair-weather vs. foul-weather sailing; or conflicting personal habits, for example, slob versus compulsively neat. To share the ownership successfully, all the parties should be compatible sailing-wise, even if they don't sail together. The various owners may also have different amounts of money to spend on the shared boat. This again can lead to conflict on outfitting, purchase of new equipment, and repairs.

Keep in mind that it is much easier to initiate than to change or dissolve a joint ownership arrangement. A good friendship isn't enough. Even if you are sharing the boat with your mother, prepare a contract that spells out in detail how scheduling, costs, repairs, and improvements will be handled.

"Time-share" arrangements, a commercial version of the partnership, can be subject to a host of additional problems. Be certain to obtain satisfactory answers to the following critical questions before you buy a share.

What is the stability of the managing organization? How long have they been in business? What prior experience do they have in this area? What is the current performance record of the managing organization on scheduling, maintenance, improvements, moorage, and so forth? Do you expect them to perform at this same level over the entire life of your time-share ownership? Are their profits made primarily on the initial sale of the boat to the time-share partnership? If so, what is their incentive to stay in business once they have sold a fleet of time-share boats?

What is the mandatory ownership period? Is it longer than the average life expectancy of the boat? Charter companies typically expect to turn over their boats every five to seven years or face making a substantial investment to restore them.

How much are the management and maintenance fees? Are there any variable use fees? Can the fees be raised? If they can't, are the fees adequate to cover all costs associated with maintenance, since it is clearly in your interest to keep the boat well maintained.

What happens if the managing company doesn't perform, or goes bankrupt? What are your rights, and what responsibilities might be shifted to you and the other owners? Can you liquidate your investment? What are your financial liabilities?

BUILDING YOUR OWN BOAT

You may realize savings of from 20 to 30 percent if you build your own boat. You will also have the opportunity to personally control the quality of your boat at every stage of construction.

Boat building is an excellent hobby/avocation if you enjoy working with tools. It offers a chance to learn a wide variety of trades, such as welding and soldering, carpentry, cabinet-making, fiberglass construction, painting, electrical work, plumbing, mechanics, and so forth. When the boat is finished, you will know exactly how all of its systems function and how to repair them. You will also have the personal satisfaction and pride of seeing your work progress to eventual completion.

Building your own boat does have a number of disadvantages. The labor involved is prodigious and may easily go into the thousands of hours—eight hundred to one thousand hours

An extreme case of deferred gratification

per ton is a good rule of thumb, and it is not uncommon for large boats to take five to fourteen years to complete. Some are never completed. Construction requires a large covered work space (not always popular with neighbors in a residential area), an assortment of good industrial grade tools (not inexpensive) and, in northern climates, heat. You also have to become a general contractor dealing with hundreds of manufacturers, wholesalers, suppliers, and fabricators for work or equipment you're unable to make yourself. You won't have the advantage of a manufacturer who can make improvements with the second or third production units. Much of what you do will be trial and error. Reconstruction of both minor and major components will not be uncommon. In the worst case, you may discover major errors in construction, design, or performance after the boat has been completed. Obviously, you can't test sail a boat you're building to find out whether you're really going to like all of its handling characteristics.

The cost savings from building your own boat may be elusive for several reasons: You have to call in experts for advice or assistance; you order materials you can't use or return; you make mistakes and have to rebuild and reconstruct; you have to rent expensive space or buy tools (or make payments on a divorce settlement because you've become a recluse); and you may work on the boat during hours you could have been earning income.

THE USED BOAT

The price of a used boat ("previously owned," in marketing language) may be substantially lower than a comparably equipped new boat because of depreciation, wear and tear, market conditions, or the seller's financial situation. A used boat may include a great deal of extra equipment. It may be extensively customized, for example, with running rigging led to the cockpit, cabinetwork, and the like. It may have special character, be one of a kind, or be a unique model that has been discontinued.

The used boat has a history: prior owners are available for interviews, the ship's log can be reviewed, and other boats of the same design may be available for comparison. If the boat has been seriously sailed, it should have been debugged and improved by the previous owners. Even if no serious flaws have been repaired, they should at least be apparent by now. If the boat has been well maintained, there should be less initial maintenance than there is with a new boat.

There are disadvantages to buying a used boat, of course. There is more "shopping" involved, such as phone calls, visiting marinas, and meeting with brokers and owners. This is because you have many more choices than with a new boat. You are looking at a package sale that includes customization and extra equipment you may neither want nor need. With a new boat you need only select the basic design and then add or subtract features. More choices and previous customization may make it harder to find the boat that meets your specific needs or dreams. Usually this means that you will have to compromise to a greater degree. You may even be paying for equipment and customizing that will interfere with future outfitting and modifications.

Have I got a deal for you.

Even if the boat has been meticulously maintained, the normal wear and tear of sailing will shorten the life of the various systems. This means that major replacements and repairs, such as for sails, the engine, keel bolts, and so forth, will probably occur earlier. Parts for older boats and their equipment may be difficult to find. This can result in expensive custom fabrication of parts.

THE NEW BOAT

Shopping for a new boat is somewhat simplified because you have fewer choices and you can look at groups of boats at dealers or boat shows. You have the potential benefit of the newest designs, materials, and technology. Of course, this is applicable only when the designer and builder incorporate new developments into their work on an ongoing basis. You can even visit the factory and see boats being constructed. Another advantage of buying a new boat is that financing is more readily available and is usually more generous. The new boat can also be equipped and customized to meet your specific needs. After the initial break-in period, maintenance should be less for the first several years.

Major disadvantages of a new boat are that it will cost more initially and will depreciate rapidly. In addition, YOU are responsible for the decisions, costs, and/or labor involved in outfitting a new boat. This process will be compressed into a relatively short time frame. Also, YOU will be debugging the boat. And every boat, no matter what its quality, will require debugging.

OWN YOUR OWN AND CHARTER IT TO OTHERS

The major advantage of buying and then chartering to others is that the costs of ownership are reduced through the charter fee and any available business tax deductions. In addition, many charter companies will handle all of the scheduling and maintenance of the boat in return for a percentage of the charter fee.

The disadvantages of chartering your own boat are several. To be successfully chartered, the boat shouldn't be too uniquely equipped or customized. You may have to compromise your own desires in order to attract the average charter sailor. The best boat for chartering will probably resemble one of those designed for and used by the large chartering operations. The boat is usually chartered "in season," when you will usually want to use it. Charter clients will cause both major and minor damage. This may be hard to accept on a boat that is near and dear to you. The boat will receive additional wear and tear from increased usage. This means more maintenance for you during the off season and a shorter life span for the boat's systems. In addition, since tax laws can have a significant impact on the financial advantages of chartering, you should seek advance advice from your accountant. Federal tax law—as well as state law—should be reviewed each year to determine current impact.

IV.

CHARACTERISTICS OF DIFFERENT TYPES OF CONSTRUCTION MATERIALS

One of the major issues in the decision process is the type of construction material for the hull and deck. The major factors in selecting a material are cost, maintenance, performance, and use. If you can eliminate several materials or focus on one type, it will immediately simplify your selection process and reduce the number of boats you must consider. While most buyers are now interested in fiberglass boats, the other available materials have characteristics that may be more suited to your specific needs. The following section discusses the primary characteristics of each type of construction material.

FIBERGLASS

Fiberglass is relatively easy to work and to mold into many different shapes. Consequently, it imposes few restrictions on the shape of the hull. It is impervious to rot, worms, or corrosion, and has a good strength to weight ratio. Fiberglass is more suitable for mass production than other materials, which frequently translates into cost savings. Although normal wear and tear is usually restricted to gelcoat crazing and fading, more serious problems are possible in a poorly constructed or maintained boat, including delamination, voids, core rot, and blistering. Fiberglass also stands up poorly to abrasion.

WOOD

Most of the older classic designs were made in wood. Now wood is commonly used for the interiors and joiner work in most boats, whatever their hull-deck construction.

Wood is an easy-to-work material using traditional woodworking tools (as well as modern electric tools) and skills. If you already have experience with wood construction through house remodeling, cabinetmaking, or furniture making, you are well on your way to being able to work on a wooden boat. For many people, wood is aesthetically pleasing and has a warmer and more traditional appearance.

Unless the boat is constructed of an epoxy laminate, the wooden boat will generally be heavier than a comparable fiberglass or aluminum boat. There is often less room inside a boat of traditional wood construction because of the space taken up by stringers, ribs, and bulkheads, and because the older designs in wood used less freeboard and lower cabin trunks. Standing headroom in older designs was rare under thirty feet LOA (length overall), and fewer bunks were generally included.

Wood requires more maintenance than most other construction materials. Major concerns are rot, surface finish, sealing of fastenings, deck leaks, hull leaks, caulking, and worms. A wooden boat has to be constantly maintained to prevent major problems. If it is not taken care of for a year or more, or tightly closed up without proper ventilation, serious problems can be expected.

The cost of a wooden boat in less than mint condition will

be substantially discounted. The price of a new wooden boat using traditional labor-intensive construction methods and top-grade wood will be comparable to or higher than the price of a new boat constructed of other materials. Financing and insurance will be harder to secure for any boat with a wooden hull.

COMPOSITES

"Composite" construction refers to the combination of several materials and techniques in a single hull or deck. The use of composites has increased dramatically, with the initiative for experimentation in this area coming from the racing fraternity. The early use of composites was in the protection of wooden hulls, but they are now more commonly used to lower overall weight and increase weight-to-strength ratios. The more common composite construction techniques include fiberglass sheathing of wooden hulls and/or decks, epoxy-saturated wood, and coring of fiberglass decks and hulls with plywood, balsa, or foam.

Fiberglass sheathing of traditional wooden hulls, decks, and cabin trunks eliminates the need for caulking and minimizes some of the potential leaks of wood construction. It almost completely eliminates the chance of worm damage to the hull. It also provides additional strength to both the hull and the deck, but at the cost of a large increase in the boat's displacement. Inspection for rot in the wood layers is much more difficult with fiberglass sheathing, as are repairs if a problem is found.

The use of *epoxy-saturated wood* has increased in the racing community considerably within the past several years. This technique is infrequently used for custom-built cruising or production boats. It produces a light boat with high strength. Unfortunately, this method is relatively expensive. Because of its comparative rarity and the layered characteristics of the construction technique, repairs may be difficult for the amateur.

Cored fiberglass uses a core material between two fiberglass skins. Cores reduce weight, increase stiffness, and provide sound and heat insulation. They can fail, rot, or separate from the fiberglass skins if quality during construction isn't high and if fittings that puncture the core aren't meticulously sealed. Almost all decks and some hulls are cored. End-grain balsa is used in the majority of decks. Plywood, high-density foam, and honeycomb are also used. Hulls are usually cored with foam or end-grain balsa, either from the sheer to the waterline or all the way to the keel. Balsa used below the waterline requires the highest standards of construction and maintenance.

STEEL

Steel-hulled and decked boats are immensely strong, providing a large safety margin in survival storms or against being holed in a collision or grounding. Few production boats are built with steel. Steel boats are usually custom-built boats or home-built to purchased plans. Above approximately forty feet LOD (length on deck), steel boats are more competitive with fiberglass boats, both in weight and in cost.

Steel construction, particularly in boats under fifty feet LOD, tends to be heavy, with high displacement-length ratios. This is because of the high weight and minimum plate thickness requirements of steel construction. Because of construction limitations and cost considerations, steel boats, particularly in the smaller designs, usually have full keels and are hard-chined (have sharp angles on the bottom where the plates meet rather than a smooth, continuous curve).

The steel boat, unless properly insulated, will have heavy condensation and will be noisy. Steel requires meticulous rust and galvanic protection. (Galvanic corrosion occurs when an electric current is created by immersing two dissimilar metals in water, particularly salt water. The metal with the higher electrical potential gives off a current that causes it to lose its molecular structure, corrode, and eventually dissolve or disappear completely.) Sophisticated compass correction is also usually required on the steel boat.

ALUMINUM

Aluminum produces a very light but strong hull with a high strength to weight ratio. Galvanic corrosion and electrolysis are serious concerns, particularly electrolysis because of the speed with which it can progress. Because of the high cost of marine-grade aluminum alloys and the sophisticated welding and plate-bending techniques required during construction, aluminum is a very expensive material. Although it is rarely used in production boats, aluminum is more common in custom work.

FERROCEMENT

A ferrocement boat is usually built from purchased plans by the home builder or as a custom design. Ferrocement boats usually have full keels and are very heavy, with high displacement-length ratios. In larger boats, however, the weight ratio becomes more comparable to other construction materials. As a rule, ferrocement hulls have a low weight-to-strength ratio.

The major cost savings (usually about 10 to 15 percent) with the ferrocement boat are in the hull material and in labor if it is home built. The deck and deckhouse are usually made of wood or wood with fiberglass sheathing. Construction costs following the hull lay-up are similar to those for wood and/ or fiberglass hulls, assuming comparable quality in the rigging, engine, hardware, and other features.

During a survey it is very difficult to ascertain the quality control used in the lay-up of the hull, unless there are obvious problem areas. The hull must use sufficient reinforcing rod (this is what gives it its strength), which must be rust-proofed. The cement plaster must be mixed correctly and have no voids. Voids or inadequate rust-proofing can result in corrosion, including galvanic corrosion, of the reinforcing rods, threatening the hull's integrity.

The resale value of ferrocement boats is low, in some instances only 50 percent of comparable boats constructed of other materials. This is because of the difficulty of ascertaining the hull's integrity in a survey and a history of poor quality control in the hull lay-up by many amateur home builders. Both of these factors have created a negative reputation for ferrocement hull boats.

V.

RIGS

The rig, or sail plan, is a critical factor in any boat's performance. The most important considerations in selecting the rig are the type of sailing you intend to do and the ease of handling and performance you expect. Following is a brief review of each type of rig, together with the primary factors that should be considered as you approach a decision.

CATS

The cat rig has a single mast stepped quite far forward in the boat, often almost at the bow. A single large sail (main) is carried behind the mast. This sail is usually attached to a long boom that extends almost back to the transom. The main may be gaff or Marconi rigged, although the more efficient Marconi sail now predominates.

The cat sail plan is theoretically the most efficient of all rigs because the sail sets in "clean" air with no turbulence from foresails and also because setting it near the boat's centerline

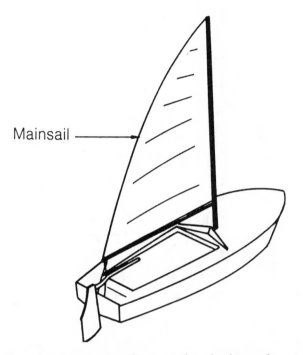

Mainsail

A single sail on a mast, usually carried in the forward section, identifies the cat. The Marconi sail has a triangular shape, giving it a longer leading edge and thus more lift to windward.

permits a close tacking angle to the true wind. In light wind conditions, however, the cat has no upwind sails beyond the main, in contrast to boats rigged with foresails, which can set deck-sweeping genoas. As the cat gets larger, this lack of versatility becomes more of a disadvantage. To support the same sail area as a boat with two or more sails, the aspect ratio (the ratio between a sail's height and width) of the cat's main must be higher (in other words, the sail must be narrow and tall). This results in a more powerful sail with a longer luff, but the stability of the boat also begins to be affected as the mast gets overly high. The main also gets too big for the crew to handle, thus

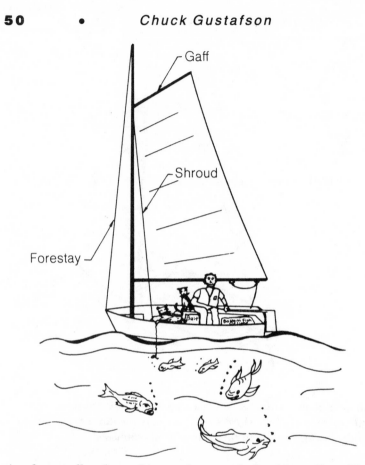

Another small catboat, this one shown with the older gaff rig. The sail in a gaff rig has an asymmetrical trapezoidal shape.

putting a practical limit on the size of a single masted cat-rigged boat (about mid-thirties LOA).

ALTERNATIVE RIGS

Since the mid-seventies some older rigs, coupled with new technology and materials, have regained their popularity. These include cats, cat ketches, and cat schooners using tapered freestanding spars (no standing rigging). The sail plans of these rigs typically consist of a single mainsail (cat), a mainsail and mizzen (cat ketch), or a mainsail and foresail (cat schooner). Recently some designers have attempted to make their boats more "mainstream" by including small fractional self-tending jibs. Although not normally seen, spinnakers and staysails can be used with these rigs for off-wind sailing if running backstays are installed. The primary advantages of these rigs are that the sail inventory is minuscule, the sails self-tending, and sail handling is reduced. A disadvantage is the lack of sail area (no option to set large genoas) for upwind work in light air. Downwind work in both light and moderate conditions suffers if spinnakers are not rigged. Other rig alternatives that may be matched with either freestanding or stayed spars include loose-footed mainsails; wishbone booms (which act as permanent vangs and self-stow the mainsail with lazy jacks); rotating cambered booms or battens; and fixed-wing sails and masts.

SLOOPS

The sloop has a single mast, carried farther aft than on the cat. Most modern sloops have the mast stayed close to the fore-and-aft centerline, permitting larger headsails to be used. The sloop normally sets two sails, a main of small to moderate size behind the mast (usually on a boom) and a jib or genoa in front of the mast from a jibstay (usually also the forestay of the boat). Although the sloop is theoretically less efficient, it is extremely versatile. It can set a wide variety of foresails, from storm jibs for survival conditions to deck-sweeping genoas for light air. It also permits splitting the sail plan to balance the boat properly and to reduce the sail area of each single sail to more manageable proportions. Because of these attributes, the modern Marconi-rigged sloop with a large foretriangle is the most popular sail plan on cruising and racing sailboats.

There are two basic types of sloops, fractional and masthead. On a *fractional* sloop, the forestay is attached to the mast at some point below the masthead. A fraction is used to describe how high off the deck the forestay is attached, with the normal range running from $3/4$ to $15/16$. As a result of the fractional attachment, jibs and genoas are smaller and the main a proportionally larger part of the drive of the boat. Rig tuning is more versatile, with extensive fore-and-aft bending of the mast possible. Tuning is also more complicated, however, and the rig often requires running backstays to support the mast where the forestay attaches.

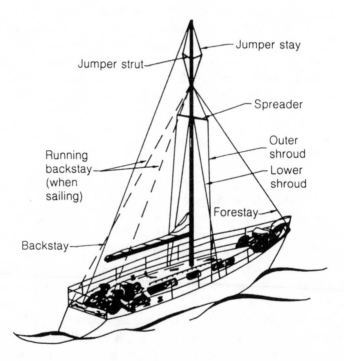

A fractional sloop has a more complicated rig than a masthead sloop. The running backstays are set tight only on the windward side and provide aft support against the forestay.

On a *masthead* sloop, the forestay attaches to the top of the mast. This rig supports larger jibs and genoas. Carried to an extreme, the main is little more than a stabilizing or balancing sail. Since this sail plan will support much larger genoas, the total potential sail area is greater than with the fractional sloop, an advantage in light wind conditions. Mast tuning is also easier with this rig.

CUTTERS

The cutter also has a single mast and a main, but it has two foresails—a staysail on an inner stay and a jib or yankee on the forestay. Many cutters can be sailed as sloops by detaching the inner stay and replacing the yankee with a large genoa. Con-

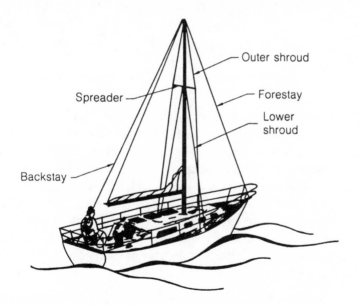

The masthead sloop carries two sails, a jib on the forestay and a main on the mast.

A cutter flying all its working sails: main, staysail, and yankee

versely, staysail sloops can set up an inner stay and carry a stay-sail. This rig won't point as high into the wind as the sloop or cat, but it offers another level of versatility since the sails are broken down into smaller increments (as a rule of thumb, the average sailor can handle a single sail in the range of three hundred to five hundred square feet). This eases sail handling and permits a wider variety of sail combinations as wind and weather conditions change. The cutter rig usually starts getting serious consideration as a boat approaches forty feet LOA if the crew is shorthanded.

YAWLS

The yawl has two masts, with the mizzen or stern mast being much smaller than the main mast and located aft of the rudder post. The yawl will not point as high as the cutter if it is rigged and sailed double-headed (as a cutter with staysail and jib). The mizzen is often backwinded when beating and when running, the mizzen can blanket either the main or one of the foresails. Because of these characteristics, knowledgeable own-

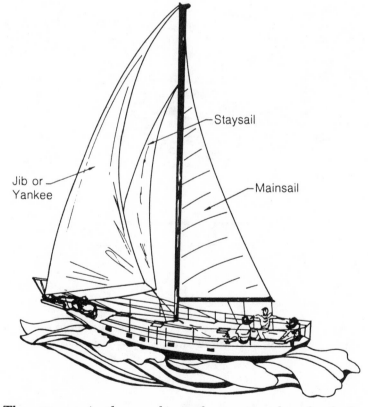

Jib or Yankee

Staysail

Mainsail

The cutter carries three working sails, a main and two headsails.

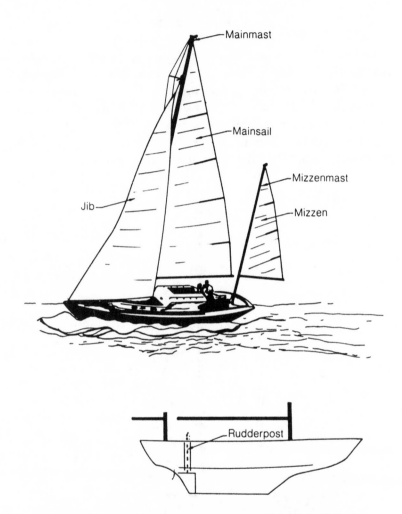

A yawl. The mizzen is usually quite small and overhangs the stern without a backstay. It is usually stepped aft of the rudder post.

ers of yawls often beat and run with the mizzen furled. Designers only credit mizzen sails at 50 percent of their area when doing performance calculations. The mizzen performs best when the boat is on a reach, particularly if a mizzen staysail or spinnaker is set. It also makes a great anchor sail by keeping the boat weather-vaned into the wind and chop. The two masts and sets of rigging make a yawl a more costly and complex alternative compared with another boat of equal sail area with a single mast.

KETCHES

The ketch also has two masts, but the mizzen is much larger than on a yawl—from 60 to 80 percent of the height of the main and located forward of the rudder post. Almost everything said about yawls applies to ketches, except that the mizzen is a much larger portion of the ketch's drive. The foresails are often rigged like a cutter, with a jib and staysail. The biggest advantage of the ketch is that it further divides the sail plan, making sail handling easier and requiring fewer sail changes.

A disadvantage not generally shared with the yawl is that the position of the mizzenmast often confuses the cockpit layout. The shorthanded crew usually begins to get seriously interested in the ketch as a boat approaches fifty feet LOA, though some energetic cruisers and single-handers have sailed cutters and even sloops up to sixty feet and longer.

SCHOONERS

The schooner has two or more masts, with the main mast the same height or higher than any of the foremasts. Again, the advantages and disadvantages are similar to those of the ketch and yawl. The schooner goes to windward more poorly than

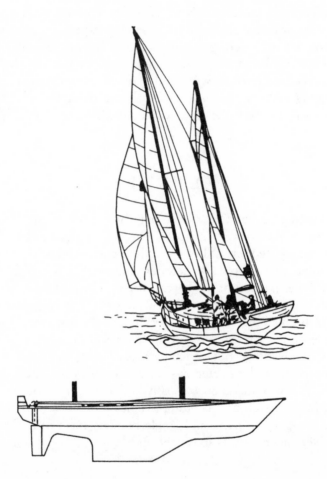

A ketch. Note that the mizzenmast is quite tall in relation to the mainmast and supports a large sail area. The mizzen is usually forward of the rudder post.

any of the rigs discussed, and the blanketing effect of the main when running is even more pronounced. The schooner can also be nasty to steer downwind, unless the main is reefed down early to balance the boat and prevent a broach. The schooner is probably the most versatile of the rigs because of the variety of sails that can be set. If only working sails are compared, it is usually superior to the other sail plans on a reach.

MOTOR SAILERS

Motor sailers can have any of the various rig configurations already discussed, but cutter and ketch rigs seem to predominate. The single most important distinction of a motor sailer is the

A schooner. Yardarm on foremast enables it to set square sails downwind.

size of its engine and the shape of the hull. Motor sailers are designed to motor more than a sailboat with an auxiliary engine. Consequently, engine size, fuel tanks, propellers, and hull shape favor motoring. Since less sailing is intended, the sail plan is usually smaller. This, of course, reduces performance under sail and provides a further incentive to motor, a potentially vicious cycle.

Motor sailers can be classified according to their engine power versus their sail power. In one system of classification the spectrum may run from the 20/80 motor sailer (with 20 percent of the characteristics of a motorboat and 80 percent of the characteristics of a sailboat) to the 80/20 motor sailer. A 20/80 motor sailer might have a sailboat hull, a moderate size sail plan, and a large engine. The 80/20 motor sailer might have a motorboat displacement hull with a very large engine

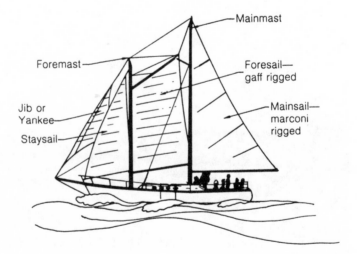

This schooner is double-headed (both jib and staysail), breaking the large area of working sail into four, more manageable sections.

(capable of speeds in excess of displacement speed) and a minimal sail plan used only for balancing the boat and helping out downwind. In addition to having less sail area, motor sailers are generally heavier than other sailboats. Their design also usually includes high freeboard, inside steering stations, and pilothouses.

In addition to performing better under power (many sailors actually power more than they sail anyway), the motor sailer usually offers more room and comfort than a true high-performance sailboat. They often make good live-aboard boats for the boater who can't completely give up sails, and in northern climates offer superior protection from the elements.

VI.

BASIC HULL, KEEL, AND RUDDER SHAPES

The hull, keel, and rudder configuration is another major decision area. Your expectations for underbody performance, safety, practicality, and aesthetics should all be matched against the type of sailing you intend to do.

MULTIHULLS

Multihulls include outriggers, catamarans, and trimarans. You probably will not be concerned with the outrigger unless you're looking for a fast, exotic daysailer. *Catamarans* have two hulls and are built as production daysailers in many sizes. There are a few production builders of cruising catamarans, as well as many home-built cats using purchased plans.

Trimarans have three hulls—a large center hull with two smaller outside hulls or sponsons. They are usually designed for cruising and are typically larger than catamarans. Most trimarans are home-built to plans.

The advantages of multihulls are several. Light weight

makes them very fast and enables them to use smaller sail plans without an appreciable performance loss in light or moderate wind conditions. Shoal draft permits them to enter shallow harbors and to be easily beached on a low tide for hull maintenance. Multihulls heel very little and provide a stable sailing and living platform. They offer a huge amount of interior and deck space at a relatively low cost per square foot. Finally, because they lack a heavy lead keel, they can be fitted with enough flotation to give them positive buoyancy.

Unfortunately, the disadvantages of multihulls are many. They are only fast if they are kept light and provided with adequate sail area. Since many cruisers load their boats down with tons of gear and then use a small, conservative sail plan, much of their speed advantage is lost. The multihull has very high initial stability but no ultimate stability. This means that in

This immaculate trimaran clearly shows the tremendous amount of deck and living space available in a large multihull.

severe conditions the boat could be flipped upside down from carrying too much sail, by catching a leeward hull, or by a rogue wave. Once flipped, the large multihulls are very stable in the inverted position. Because of their high degree of windage they point poorly, tend to yaw and sail around their anchors, and can be difficult to bring into a tight anchorage or dock if there is any wind blowing. Their size also makes fitting into the average marina berth rather unlikely.

MONOHULLS

Monohulls, a broad category, includes all boats with a single hull—from light, shallow planing hulls to deep, heavy displacement hulls. Like multihulls, monohulls come in a variety of sizes, from six-foot prams to eighty-foot luxury yachts.

Monohulls with light, shallow planing hulls are usually referred to as having a *dinghy hull.* Most tenders to larger boats, day sailers, and small one-design racing sailboats have dinghy hull shapes. This shape is now used on almost all new racing boats and in the majority of new racer-cruisers. The dinghy hull has a shallow draft, sometimes measured in inches, which enables it to sail shallow lakes and rivers and to be easily beached, trailered, and launched from docks. The lay-up of the hull involves less material, thus reducing costs. The dinghy hull is a lighter hull, making it generally easier to handle. Light, shallow, and flat, the dinghy hull moves easily in light airs and gets up on a plane quickly, producing high downwind speeds. The relatively flat bottom causes pounding when going to windward. In boats intended for cruising, it produces less displacement (for interior accommodations, stores, fuel, and water).

The larger racing and day-sailing boats with dinghy hull shapes rely on a weighted keel to produce stability, to give the boat a self-righting capability, and to increase its ability to carry sail. The smaller daysailers and one-design racers utilize a centerboard or daggerboard to provide lateral stability, enabling the boat to track and sail to windward. While centerboards and daggerboards work well for that purpose, they don't provide ultimate stability, and if the boat is heeled over too far it can lay on its side or even turn turtle without righting itself. Then it is up to the crew to right the boat, which hopefully has enough positive flotation to prevent it from sinking.

Sailboats with deeper, heavier hull shapes are said to have *displacement hulls*. With more weight and wetted surface, and a larger bow wave, this hull is slower in light air and less likely to surf on a wave. For most purposes the speed of this hull shape is limited to its displacement or hull speed. More room is available for accommodations, stores, and equipment, which are important on larger boats used for overnight trips and cruising. While the initial stability of this hull shape is not as high as that of the true dinghy hull, it increases as the boat heels. To provide even more stability and a self-righting capability, weight in the form of ballast is attached to the bottom of the keel. If everything has been designed correctly the boat shouldn't turn turtle, and if it does, it should right itself. Because of the enormous weight of the ballast (typically 30 to 50 percent of the boat's total displacement), it is not usually possible to have positive flotation. Consequently, if the displacement keel boat is holed, it will quickly sink unless the water can be removed or the leak stopped.

CENTERBOARDS AND DAGGERBOARDS

Centerboards and daggerboards are usually used on sailboats up to around twenty feet LOA to provide stability and lateral resistance. After twenty feet, weighted keels become more prevalent.

Centerboards are raised or lowered on a hinge with a winch or block and tackle. When not in use, they are stored in a centerboard trunk, an enclosed slit in the keel or bottom of the hull. With the centerboard down, the boat has increased lateral resistance (resistance to being pushed sideways) and substantially improved windward performance. With the board almost all the way up, the boat has decreased wetted surface for better downwind performance. In the various positions in between full up and full down, the board can be used to help balance the boat and obtain the ultimate possible performance. Changing the position of the board moves the center of the lateral plane fore and aft to match the movement of the center of effort caused by different sail combinations and sail trim. With the centerboard up, the boat also has a greatly reduced draft, enabling it to be beached or to enter very shoal harbors.

The centerboard does have some disadvantages, however. The trunk can clutter the cockpit or cabin; the centerboard may bang; and the trunk may gurgle, spit, or even leak. The centerboard can also jam up or down. On larger boats, where it is used to create shoal draft, the centerboard will increase the cost, maintenance, and complexity of the boat.

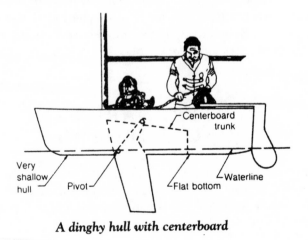

A dinghy hull with centerboard

Daggerboards are raised or lowered straight up and down through a narrow trunk or slot in the hull. They serve the same purpose as the centerboard, but with less mechanics. Because they aren't hinged, however, they are much more apt to be damaged in grounding, and they present more of a storage problem. Daggerboards, although common on small dinghies, are rarely seen on larger boats.

There are many variations and combinations of the centerboard, daggerboard, and keel. Common combinations include the weighted centerboard or daggerboard and the fixed weighted keel with a centerboard trunk inside it.

KEELS

Keels come in many shapes. While they all provide lateral resistance to enable the sailboat to track and sail to windward, they represent significant differences in performance. Traditional *full keels* run the entire length of the bottom of the hull. In some cases they blend into the hull so completely that they are indistinguishable from the deep, heavy displacement hull to which they are usually matched. Modern hull and keel design has borrowed heavily from aerodynamics. Close examination of a modern keel reveals its similarity to the foil section of an airplane wing. Modern keels perform much better than their historical counterparts, which were drawn by eye and to traditional lines. There is a high probability that the full keel will not be a modern foil section since most full keels are older designs or newer copies of older designs. The design restrictions of the full keel on a very deep hull also make production of a good foil section difficult, since the keel often has a low aspect ratio and is broadly faired into the hull at the root (top of the keel).

Two improvements were made to the full keel that greatly enhanced its performance. One was to cut away part of the forefoot (hull underbody at the bow), and the other was to

A full-keel fiberglass boat. The large outboard hung rudder should partially compensate for the lack of cutaway at the forefoot, although the propeller aperture will degrade the rudder's performance.

remove part of the keel at the stern section. Both of these changes reduced wetted surface and weight. Cutting away the forefoot improved the steering responsiveness and ease of tacking.

A major advantage of the full keel boat is that it usually tracks well, holding a course with little rudder action. It also hauls out or careens for maintenance easily. Matched with a deep hull and heavy displacement, as it so often is, the keel provides room for water and fuel tanks deep in the hull and in the upper part of the keel, where their weight is best placed. The disadvantages are primarily in performance. The full keeled boat will have a high wetted-surface area, will be heavier, and consequently will be slower. Although it will track well, it will not be as responsive to the helm, will be more difficult to tack, and may not steer well in close quarters maneuvering. Finally, it will generally not point as high because it lacks the lift that comes from a modern foil-section keel.

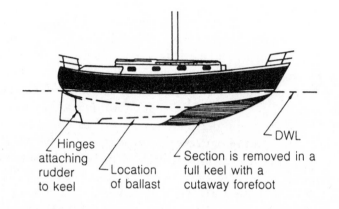

Hinges attaching rudder to keel

Location of ballast

Section is removed in a full keel with a cutaway forefoot

DWL

A typical shape for a full keel. As the forefoot is cut away, the boat becomes more maneuverable.

A moderately high-aspect fin keel. The moderately high-aspect rudder is mounted on a partial skeg.

Fin keels are essentially vertical wings. Referred to as having a foil shape, their leading edge is thicker than their trailing edge. Fins are typically matched with light displacement hulls with a shallow, dinghy-type shape. With high aspect ratios, the ratio of depth (span) to length (chord), fins usually have more lift and can point higher than keels with low ratios. The fin keel will usually have less wetted surface, which will improve boat speed in light air. Fins are quick turning and fast tacking.

Fin keels generally do not track as well as full keels, with tracking deteriorating as aspect ratio increases. The stress on the keel bolts of a high aspect ratio fin makes the engineering and assembly of the keel attachment critical. Fin keel boats are hard to haul out without a Travelift, careening is difficult, and grids may be impossible to use. In an accidental grounding, the boat may heel to dangerously extreme angles.

Fins come in many variations: elliptical, whale fin, Collins Tandem, bulb or torpedo, Scheel, and wing. I particularly like the Scheel keel, because it is simple and effective, but reduces draft. A note of caution: Be aware that the wing keel may act like an anchor if you go aground in a soft bottom.

RUDDERS

Like keels, rudders come in many shapes and are attached in several locations.

Keel hung rudders offer superior protection in a grounding or collision. They also dampen the steering, which results in better tracking under conditions that make steering difficult. Unfortunately, the dampening effect makes them less effective when turning in close quarters. Further, a keel hung rudder doesn't provide a separate foil. Since the leading edge of the keel or rudder is what gives it most of its windward lift, a separate foil-shaped rudder improves the windward performance of a boat.

A moderately high-aspect fin keel with medium sweepback angle to the leading edge

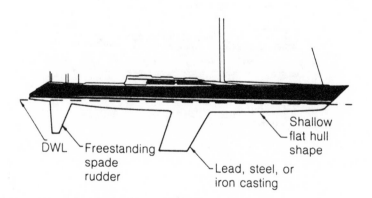

A high-aspect fin keel and spade rudder on a large lightweight ocean racer

Spade rudders are freestanding foil sections (again, like an airplane wing) attached to the hull only by the rudder shaft. Like fin keels, they have aspect ratios with similar performance characteristics. While spade rudders provide excellent responsiveness and turning characteristics, the boat can develop "squirrelly" steering downwind and require constant helm attention. This problem is magnified as rudder and keel aspect ratios increase. The rudder is also under more stress and is more at risk in a grounding or from logs and debris.

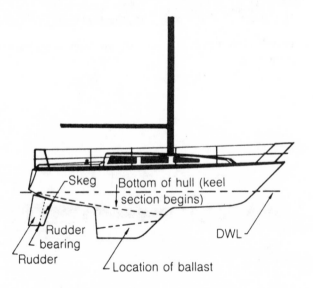

A popular compromise between the full and extreme fin keels is the low to moderate fin keel with a skeg of varying size. This shape combines much of the tracking performance of the full keel with maneuverability that is close to that of the spade rudder.

Skeg hung rudders are a compromise between spade rudders and keel hung rudders. A skeg is a small isolated section of keel with a large cutaway in front of it, aft of a fin keel. Skegs come in various sizes and shapes, but they all dampen the steering, improve tracking ability, provide protection for the rudder, and strengthen the attachment of the rudder by linking it to the

A high-aspect spade rudder with a very small skeg. Note the blistering, a common problem with fiberglass hulls.

skeg. The skeg configuration has less wetted surface than the full keel and provides another foil section for improved lift to windward. Combining a skeg hung rudder with a moderate aspect ratio fin keel makes a nice compromise between the high aspect spade rudder and fin keel and the traditional full keel. This configuration is now seen quite often on what are being called "performance cruisers."

Outboard hung rudders may be fastened to a full keel or a skeg or be freestanding like a spade rudder. Attached to the transom, they bring the rudder back to the farthest point aft, increasing its relative power. Tillers and self-steering vanes are

This high-aspect rudder is hung from a small but full-length skeg. Note the bearing at the bottom of the skeg, which supports the rudder.

easier to install on the outboard rudder, and inspections and repairs are facilitated by its accessibility. They are more susceptible to damage, however, because of their location.

STERNS

Many of my students ask about the characteristics of different types of sterns. There are four basic types, with many variations and combinations.

This outboard rudder with tiller is both transom and keel hung. The large open slot between the rudder and keel and the propeller aperture will create turbulence and reduce the effectiveness of the rudder.

One type is the *counter stern,* which can overhang the waterline either moderately or extremely. This stern provides reserve buoyancy, which reduces the probability of being pooped by a large following sea, and additional waterline when the boat is sailing beyond its displacement speed. It also provides a

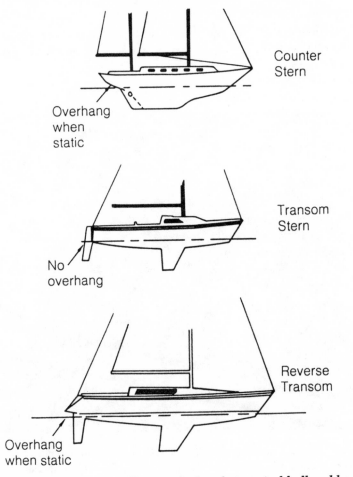

Three different stern profiles matched to their typical hull and keel shapes

higher proportion of deck space for a given waterline, perhaps providing an aft deck for sunning or an attachment point for backstays without resorting to a boomkin (which is basically a stern bowsprit). A locker aft of the cockpit (lazaret) is also usually available for additional storage. One disadvantage of this stern is that if heavily loaded, particularly if the overhang is extreme, it will increase "hobby-horsing" (the fore-and-aft, up-and-down movement of the boat) in a seaway. The overhang also increases the cost of construction slightly for a specific waterline length.

The *transom stern* is cut off nearly flat or straight from the deck to the waterline. It is very common on dinghies, small day sailers, and pocket cruisers. If cut off before the beam is severely pinched, this stern creates large buoyant aft sections that contribute to the boat's ability to get up on a plane downwind. It also creates a larger cockpit and more storage in the cockpit lockers.

The *reverse transom* brings the hull out beyond the deck and cockpit at the waterline so that it points aft, inversely to the angle of the bow. This is commonly done on racing boats and in moderation on some cruiser-racers. The transom is reversed to gain additional waterline length with a minimal gain in weight and cost. In its extreme forms, it may make anchoring, docking, or tying up a dinghy from the stern difficult. Installation of equipment such as swim ladders and self-steering vanes may also be a problem.

The last group of sterns that are of interest include the *double-ender* (also known as the *Colin Archer* or *Scandinavian*) and the *canoe*. The former is usually found on full keel boats, while the latter may be used with a variety of hull and keel shapes. Despite almost incredible claims of seaworthiness, these sterns are probably no better than other types. Many of the myths about canoe and double-ender sterns developed because they were used on pilot boats and small sailboats that were successfully sailed in severe conditions and were later written about by their survivors. These boats were close to "state of the art" when they made their reputations, but design and construction have further evolved and many seaworthy designs are now available. The only clear claim that I can substantiate is that these sterns are very appealing aesthetically.

On the other side is a string of disadvantages. If carried to an extreme and matched to a full keel, as on a Colin Archer type, these sterns may be seriously lacking in buoyancy in the aft sections. Narrower aft sections also make the cockpit more cramped and reduce cockpit locker space. The earlier and the more severely the stern is pinched, the greater will be the reduction in the volume of the entire boat. The extremely pinched stern will also be less apt to get out of the trough behind the bow wave and surf when running or reaching.

The stern of this double-ender looks remarkably like a bow.

VII.

PERFORMANCE CRITERIA

"Performance criteria" are the bench data that describe the boat's design characteristics and anticipated performance levels. They are useful because they permit you to compare on paper the sailing performance of a large number of boats in order to narrow the selection field. They are also useful for specific boat evaluations, since they provide data that could only be replicated by sailing the boat over a lengthy period in every conceivable weather condition.

A few of the criteria are best obtained using estimates or eyeball judgments. For most of the criteria, however, specific numbers are used to compare a specific boat both with "normal ranges" for all boats and with other boats in your decision pool. Most of the performance data are available in published boat reviews, in the boat's specs, or from the designer, builder, dealer, or broker. The majority of the criteria are also fairly easy to compute, although a few require a scientific calculator.

It is usually best to narrow your choices on construction material, rig and sail plan, and hull-keel-rudder before applying the performance criteria. By making these basic design decisions early, you are more likely to compare boats that are roughly similar. Trying to compare dissimilar designs, such as a light summer cruiser with an Arctic waters steel boat, is like comparing double chocolate Häagen-Dazs with broccoli.

Designers use a wide range of performance criteria. I have tried to select those that are the most critical to sailboat selection, while not being overwhelmingly technical. As your expertise grows, you will want to add and subtract from the suggested criteria. All the criteria discussed in this chapter are listed in the Performance Criteria Checklist, Appendix C, which is designed to be used as a worksheet.

WATERLINE LENGTH (LWL)

There are three different measures for the length of a sailboat. LOA (length overall) is supposed to include all significant overhangs that are a permanent part of the boat, such as bowsprits, anchor platforms, and boomkins. LOD (length on deck) is the measure down the center of the deck without including overhangs. Sometimes the boat's specs will confuse LOA and LOD and fail to include all overhangs in LOA. LWL (length at the waterline) is the centerline measure of the boat's static waterline. A moving boat will squat in the water, immersing more of the hull and increasing the "effective waterline." Of the three measures of length, LWL is the best at describing the boat's performance.

Sailboats, particularly heavy boats with deep hulls and full keels, usually move at displacement speeds. An amount of water equal to that displaced by the hull is replaced at the stern as the boat moves through the water. As speed increases, resistance to the boat's forward motion also increases, and the hull creates a deeper hole between the bow and the stern waves. Proportionally larger increases in power (engine or sail) are required to increase boat speed. An extremely heavy boat with a

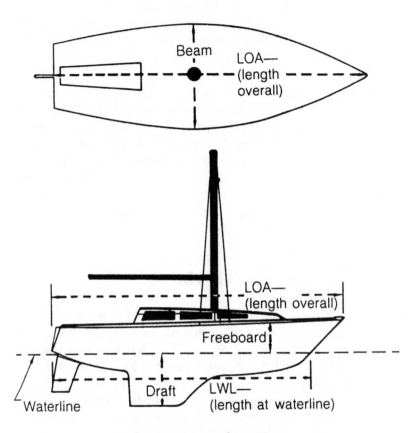

Some important dimensions

deep hull form and inadequate reserve buoyancy could theoretically become a submarine if enough power were available. This
happens when the bow wave displaces more water than can be
replaced by the stern wave. A few people believe that this is
how some of the clipper ships were lost.

To exceed hull speed, the boat must either surf down a

wave or plane to get out of the wave trough. Most hull forms will surf if wave and wind conditions are right. Light boats with shallow dinghy-like hulls are most likely to surf and are the only hull forms that will actually plane.

When a boat is sailing in a displacement mode, the LWL is the primary constraint on boat speed. To calculate the maximum practical displacement hull speed, multiply 1.34 times the square root of the LWL. 1.34 is the speed-length ratio selected by designers as an arbitrary dividing line. Above 1.34 a typical displacement hull must surf or plane to attain higher speeds or the boat must have tremendous power available from sail or engine. To estimate realistic boat speeds for passage planning purposes, use a speed-length ratio of 1 in the formula instead of 1.34.

BEAM

Beam is the maximum width of the boat. Unless the boat has tumblehome (when the widest part of the boat is between the waterline and the sheerline and the hull has a convex shape), maximum beam will be at deck level. For best all-around performance, beam should be moderate. Increasing beam gives the hull greater initial resistance to heeling (called "form stability") and enlarges the boat's interior. Excessive beam can result in a loss of directional stability, severe weather helm in heavy conditions, pounding, an increase in form resistance (drag), and low ultimate stability.

The ratio of beam to LOD (beam divided by LOD) provides a measure of relative beam (never tell a sailor his/her boat is fat). A ratio of .33 or less is a good design objective. Boats with higher ratios may sail just fine but should receive extra scrutiny. Sometimes an excessively beamy boat has been designed to sell an interior rather than for sailing performance. Remember you're buying a SAILboat, not an apartment.

DRAFT

Draft is the amount of water required to float the boat without going aground. Centerboard and daggerboard boats have two drafts—board up and board down. The draft of your boat can be critical when anchoring in a small cove, motoring in a canal or river, or when sailing in regions with extensive shoal areas, such as the Gulf Coast, Florida, Chesapeake Bay, the Bahamas, the canals of France, and so forth. It is very important for trailer sailers, since as draft increases, trailering, launching, and recovering of the boat become more difficult. The trailer sailer with a deep draft will be restricted to far fewer ramp locations. On the other hand, as fixed draft is reduced, ability to sail close to the wind deteriorates rapidly, unless a Scheel or wing keel, centerboard, or the like has been added to compensate.

Shoal draft is a relative term meaning that the boat has optional keels, one deep and one shoal (shallow), or that the boat draws relatively less water than other boats of its type. For instance, a boat that is considered to have a shoal draft on Puget Sound would have a comparatively deep draft for the Gulf Coast or Florida.

WINDAGE

The wind is continually exerting pressure on the topsides, cabin trunk, rigging, and deck equipment. All these surfaces, with the exception of raised sails, are said to have *windage*. Boats with extensive surface area above the waterline in relation to their size are said to have excessive windage. These boats like to sail around their anchors, making skippers and crew of neighboring boats nervous. They are more difficult to dock and maneuver in close quarters, since the wind overwhelms the boat's normal handling characteristics. Finally, they will be slower upwind and more difficult to tack. Excessive windage is

This older wooden racer/cruiser has a very low profile with a cabin trunk just high enough for small windows. This boat could be expected to have low windage.

like having an extra sail up *backwards*, all the time. Many modern designs have high freeboard and cabins to obtain better headroom. This is often not compatible with good sailing performance. In small boats you can often improve performance dramatically by opting for good sitting headroom instead of standing headroom.

There are two easy ways to estimate windage. The quick and dirty method is to measure the freeboard at the stern and the bow. The bow measure is the most important since windage here has the most impact. A more accurate estimate of windage is obtained by calculating the approximate surface area of one side of the boat. (Don't worry about overhangs—assume a rectangular shape.) Measure the freeboard at its lowest point (usually about amidships near the shrouds) and multiply by LOD. Then multiply the height of the cabin trunk and/or pilothouse by its length. Add the two totals together. Now eyeball the

No measuring tape is necessary to realize that this boat has lots of freeboard and hence windage.

rigging, deck gear, and the like, and add a "clutter factor." This might be from 5 to 20 percent of your base figure for the hull and cabin. Compare the windage of the boats under consideration using either of these methods, but remember that the boats should be of similar displacement and length for a comparison to be meaningful.

DISPLACEMENT

Displacement is the weight of the volume of water displaced by the hull. As total displacement increases, seaworthiness and motion improve. The amount of living space also increases, and the boat can carry more provisions, water, fuel, spare parts, and luxury, convenience, and safety equipment. The dollar costs, maintenance, and complexity, however, rise at a geometric rate with increasing displacement. The gear also gets harder to physically handle, particularly when the inevitable equipment breakdown occurs.

One way to analyze displacement is to estimate your minimum requirements for stowage, living space, and comfort in pounds of displacement. Then select a waterline based on what you would like in a displacement-length ratio (discussed below). Be aware that the displacement numbers given with the boat specs are often questionable, due to poor quality control during construction and changes by the builder and owners. All these errors often result in a boat that is overweight. I recently

A mast that has been tapered for the last 20 percent or so of its length

worked on a steel boat that weighed 40 percent over its designed displacement.

BALLAST-DISPLACEMENT RATIO

This is a crude measure of initial stability, since it does not take into account form stability or center of gravity (for example, deep keel versus a shoal keel). It is calculated by dividing the weight of the ballast by the total displacement. The range for this ratio is very broad, but most boats cluster between .3 and .5. If everything else is equal, a high ratio means higher stability.

A variation on this ratio is used to determine usable displacement for living aboard. The ballast helps sail the boat but is useless for living space or storing equipment, provisions, and so forth. Subtract the ballast from the total displacement, leaving "liveaboard displacement."

DISPLACEMENT-LENGTH RATIO

The displacement-length ratio describes the RELATIVE weight of boats with different LWLs and displacements. It is calculated as follows: displacement-length ratio = displacement in long tons (2,240 lb./long ton) divided by [(.01 × LWL) cubed]. Displacement-length ratios have been moving lower with more advanced construction techniques, as have our definitions of heavy and light boats. Roughly, though, we can divide displacement-length ratios into the following categories: over 400—tanks, over 300—heavy, 220 to 280—moderate, under 200—light, under 100—ULDBs (ultralight displacement boats).

Boats with high ratios are less affected by loading than boats with low ratios. Boats with high ratios will have a slower mo-

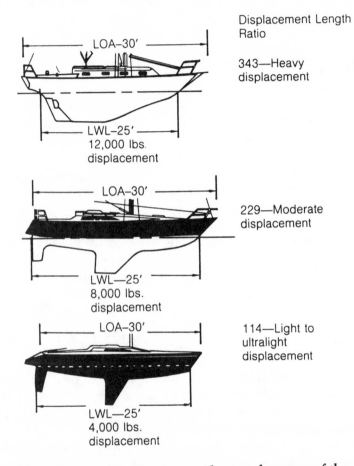

The displacement-length ratio provides a good measure of the relative heaviness of different boats.

tion in a seaway and will be better able to drive through sloppy seas in light wind. In light to moderate winds, they will require a larger sail plan to sail as well as boats with low ratios. High ratio boats need reserve buoyancy (overhangs at the bow and stern and high freeboard) or they will be wet to sail.

Boats in the ULDB category can be expensive per pound (the inverse of the typical relationship), since exotic and high tech construction is normally used. Boats with low ratios will surf and plane earlier in less wind and consequently will have higher speeds off the wind. Smaller sail plans are needed on low ratio boats, which translates into ease of sail handling and lower costs. Finally, boats with low ratios will be drier but will have a corky, bobbing motion.

WEIGHT ALOFT

Excess weight above the waterline raises the boat's center of gravity. The result is an increase in rolling and in heel under sail, plus pitching if the excess weight is distributed fore and aft. This causes the boat to be slower, wetter, and generally more uncomfortable. The higher the weight is located above the waterline, the more pronounced the effect.

Ideally, weight should be kept as low as possible when designing, building, and equipping a boat. Some of the major factors contributing to a high center of gravity include massive telephone pole masts on some imported boats, large mast mounted radar antennae, high topsides (area between waterline and deck), large pilothouses, and stowing water or fuel on deck. Some of the ways that the center of gravity can be lowered include storing heavy equipment, provisions, and spares as low in the boat as possible, keeping storm anchors in the bilge until needed, storing the chain in the bilge during a passage, installing a tapered mast, mounting the lightest equipment on the mast (for example, aluminum instead of stainless maststeps), and installing water and fuel tanks below the cabin sole.

Because weight aloft is so heavily influenced by outfitting and storage, I prefer to describe it without using numbers, rating the boat as either poor, average, or excellent.

WEIGHT IN THE ENDS

Excess weight in the ends of a boat increases pitching. This is similar to the effect of a teeter-totter. The boat's motion will be less comfortable, and forward way will be slowed. Observing a variety of boats at their moorings on a rough day will readily demonstrate differences in pitching. Weight should be carried in the center of the boat as much as possible. Some of the major offenders include long and heavy overhangs on boats with short waterlines for their LOA, inboard engines installed way aft under the cockpit sole, and water tanks under V-berths. Some of the ways to center weight include moving chain lockers as far aft as possible, installing engines forward (perhaps in the main salon), installing tanks in the central part of the boat, and keeping heavy stowage out of the stern and especially out of the bow.

As with weight aloft, it is more useful to rate weight in the ends as poor, average, or excellent.

SAIL AREA-DISPLACEMENT RATIO

This ratio represents the relationship between sail area and displacement. It provides an easy way to compare the relative sailing "horsepower" of different boats. In light conditions, hull-generated drag (friction and turbulence) and total sail area are the primary determinants of boat speed. As wind speed increases, friction is less of a factor and the total sail area available becomes more significant, because the power requirements to approach and/or exceed hull speed (see discussion on LWL) are rapidly accelerating. In heavy wind, the sail area-displacement ratio is insignificant, since any boat except the most underrigged motor sailer will have plenty of sail.

The ratio is calculated as follows: sail area-displacement ratio = sail area divided by the displacement in cubic feet (64.2

pounds of displacement equals one cubic foot) to the 2/3 power (square and then take the cube root). Values of this ratio usually range between 10 and 20 for cruising boats, with high performance dinghies and racing boats having ratios in the 20's. Boats with ratios under 12 will do a lot of motoring and will be sailing slugs unless it is blowing hard. Boats with ratios under 15 will find it hard to sail in light conditions, unless they maximize their light air sail inventory and have a mirror smooth bottom. Remember that this ratio is based on the designer's often optimistic calculation of displacement. The "real" sail area-displacement ratio will be lower (and the displacement-length ratio higher), if the boat is built overweight and/or overloaded with structural modifications, equipment, provisions, water, and fuel. This effect is most pronounced on boats designed with low displacement-length ratios.

SAIL ASPECT RATIO

Performance, particularly to windward, is enhanced by high aspect ratio sail plans. The longer luff of a high aspect sail generates more drive when going to weather. The sail is also higher off the water than its low-aspect counterpart, putting sail area into faster and less turbulent (cleaner) air. The high aspect sail plan has a higher mast capable of carrying larger light air sails. The high aspect sail plan also has a higher center of effort, which reduces apparent stability and may require earlier reefing and more frequent sail changes. The aspect ratio is calculated by dividing the height of the sail (in sailmaker's jargon, P for the main and I for the genoa) by the length of the sail's foot (E for the main and J for the jib). Ratios cluster around 3 for many modern production boats, but may be lower on older boats or higher on racing boats.

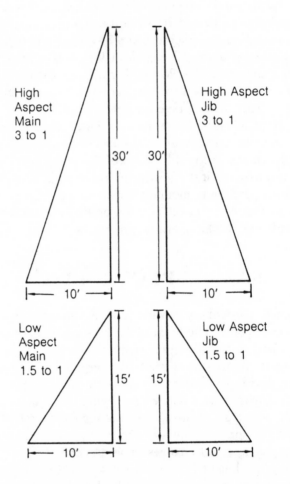

High
Aspect
Main
3 to 1

30'

High Aspect
Jib
3 to 1

30'

|— 10' —|

|— 10' —|

Low
Aspect
Main
1.5 to 1

15'

Low Aspect
Jib
1.5 to 1

15'

|— 10' —|

|— 10' —|

A high-aspect ratio sail plan can be expected to be faster and point higher when on the wind than a low-aspect sail plan. Off the wind, total projected sail area is the most important factor in boat speed.

RANGE OF POSITIVE STABILITY

The range of positive stability indicates the maximum angle of heel (measured in degrees) at which the boat will remain upright rather than roll over or capsize. This is difficult to calculate and I would suggest obtaining it from the designer or purchasing USYRU performance data. The Society of Naval Architects and Marine Engineers (SNAME)/United States Yacht Racing Union (USYRU) Joint Committee on Safety from Capsize recommends 120° as the minimum value for a range of positive stability for offshore sailing (findings are summarized in *Desirable and Undesirable Characteristics of Offshore Yachts*; see the recommended books in Chapter I). 120° was selected as the cutoff for offshore boats because, on the average, a boat with this positive stability value, if it rolls over, will remain inverted for two minutes, the maximum that a crew could be expected to hold their breath prior to righting. Boats with low positive stability, in addition to being more prone to rolling over, stay inverted longer. The higher the range of positive stability, the less likely the boat will roll over, and once over, the faster it will turn back to a normal upright position. Hull forms that resist capsize include a wineglass shape with a narrow beam-length ratio, a moderate or long keel, and a boat with balanced bow and stern sections. The mast also adds to the boat's stability, since more than one half of a typical boat's inertial moment is in the mast, a good argument for an overbuilt and well-maintained mast.

The *capsize screen* is a rough calculation when you don't know the range of positive stability. The cut off is 2, with below 2 being more stable and above 2 being less stable. It is calculated as follows: capsize screen = beam divided by the cube root of displacement in cubic feet (64.2 pounds/cubic foot).

ANALYZING PERFORMANCE CRITERIA

A specific boat's ranking relative to other boats will vary for each individual criterion. While the comparison of a single performance criterion is helpful in simplifying your analysis, one criterion can never adequately describe a boat's potential performance characteristics and should never be the sole basis for making your selection. For instance, Boat A might have the highest displacement-length ratio, which by itself would indicate a potentially slow boat. This same boat, however, might have the best weight distribution. Depending upon your selection prerequisites, this may partially or totally compensate for the boat's heavy displacement. Assume you are interested in a "performance cruiser" with a high sail area-displacement ratio. Several of the boats you are considering have ratios of 17 to 20. Boat X with a ratio of 15.5, however, might better meet your requirements because of a better ranking on draft, beam-length ratio, windage, and range of positive stability. Your interpretation of the criteria and the ranking of boats is directly related to your individual requirements and projected use of the boat. For instance, if you are racing, you will normally want a deeper keel. If you are cruising in the Bahamas, you may be willing to trade off upwind performance to reduce the time you spend aground.

When reviewing performance criteria, always be wary of boats with extreme characteristics, unless you are very knowledgeable and have specialized requirements for the boat's design. Some extremes I would be careful of include small boats with seven feet of headroom that look like house trailers; boats with a beam approaching 40 percent of their length; boats with displacement-length ratios over 400; and boats with sail area-displacement ratios under 12.

If you are having trouble deciding what to make of the performance criteria for a group of boats, keep in mind that this is only one aspect of your decision. The data are most useful in narrowing your choices and providing indicators on how you might expect the boat to perform. Before your final selection, you should always confirm what the performance criteria indicate by considering the reports of owners and the reputation of the designer's boats and by lengthy chartering or test sails if possible.

VIII.

SELF-SURVEY CRITERIA FOR THE BASIC BOAT

If you have followed this guide step by step, you will already have defined the personal and financial constraints that will influence your choice of a boat. These should be in the form of a written list that will be modified and "fine-tuned" as you look at sailboats. By now you should have selected a basic construction material for your boat and should have narrowed your choices on the type of sail plan and hull-keel-rudder configuration. You should also have reviewed a number of boats against the designers' "bench" performance data.

Now you are at the stage where you are seriously looking at individual boats. You are walking through them, looking into corners with a flashlight, standing under them, talking to owners and dealers, and trying to envision sailing, living on, and equipping each contender. You have questions about safety, quality, convenience, comfort, repairability, and performance. This and the following four chapters set forth specific criteria that you can use as standards when inspecting a sailboat. You do not need to be a surveyor or a shipwright to make valid judgments about the quality and utility of a sailboat. You do need to carefully review the construction and outfitting of each area and system on each boat in which you're seriously interested.

One thing you must keep in mind as you review Chapters VIII through XII is that you must match the construction characteristics and quality of the boat with your intended utilization, finances, and personal preferences. I have tried to emphasize the characteristics of construction, installation, and outfitting that I believe represent high quality, but you will never find one boat that meets *all* of your needs or includes *all* of these attributes. Your ideal boat, or the one that best fits your needs, will always be different from the ideal of other sailors, including mine. The ideal boat represents a changing set of requirements. If you could build it, the day you stepped aboard you would start a list of improvements based on your changing needs and the development of new technologies and equipment. The most you can expect is to find a sailboat that meets more of your requirements than any of the other boats you have considered during a reasonably thorough search. You will always have a list of modifications and equipment necessary to bring the boat up to your particular needs. You will have to accept certain trade-offs, inconveniences, and less than optimal performance—all resulting from the compromises required by your utilization plans, your financial constraints, and the particular boat you have selected.

Some examples may help illustrate this compromise process. Example One: You would really like a number ten plus quality (on a ten-point scale), highly customized boat. Because you intend to resell or trade the boat within two years, however, you buy a number five quality boat popular in your sailing area and you add no extra equipment or custom features. Example Two: You dream about sailing around the world on a fully outfitted blue-water boat. But the reality is that you are short on cash and will probably be restricted to intermittent fair-weather summer day sails with a few weekend trips on protected waters.

You could charter a boat for less than ownership costs, but you are tired of renting and want your own starter boat. You end up buying a small number four quality, simply equipped pocket cruiser. Example Three: You buy a good quality thirty-foot cruising boat. After sailing and outfitting it extensively, you still would like a few more features, such as an anchor winch, all-chain anchor rode, refrigeration, diesel stove with oven, and a hard-bottom sailing dinghy. You decide, however, that this equipment is out of scale for the size and weight of your boat. Consequently, you sail without it until you can buy a new boat large enough to accommodate your desired gear and equipment.

An entire book could have been written on each of the systems covered in these self-survey chapters. The material has been restricted, however, to the most significant criteria that are relevant to sailboat selection. Appendix D, Self-Survey Criteria Checklist for Buying a Sailboat, is a suggested format for listing your primary criteria and summarizing and ranking your findings when evaluating one or more boats. Appendix H, Sailboat Evaluation Checklist, is the guide that I use when I perform a full inspection of a boat.

SAMPLE INDICATORS OF QUALITY

You can make a fairly quick judgment, without being a naval architect or marine engineer, about the overall quality of a boat by reviewing a few sample indicators. When weight is not a consideration, hardware should be bronze, chromed bronze, or stainless steel rather than anodized aluminum. Brass should never be used for any working hardware. Wood should have a dull sheen, with no checks, cracks, or stains. Fiberglass surfaces should be fair and smooth. All work and installations should be neatly done. Surfaces under bunks, behind drawers, and in lockers and the dark corners of bins should be finished and painted. You should not see any jagged fiberglass, splintered raw wood, fiberglass dust, sawdust, dirt, lost tools, or the remnants of someone's lunch. The bilge should be clean and painted and should smell fresh. On a used boat, pull off a winch drum. The gears, pawls, and springs should be uncorroded, clean and *lightly* covered with grease. A boat that doesn't measure up to these standards will generally have other inadequacies that may be more difficult to assess or locate.

KEELS AND BALLAST

Ballast may be concrete, iron, steel, or lead. Lead is generally preferred because it has the highest density (provides a lower center of gravity), is almost inert in seawater, and is relatively easy to mold. It is also the most expensive choice. Ballast may be carried inside the hull but is more typically placed entirely within the keel.

Internal hull ballast was extensively used in older boats that depended upon their hull form for most of their stability. It will still appear occasionally in a newer boat as an easy correction to a stability problem or in a racing boat to change its rating. Internal ballast is dangerous, however, because it can come loose in a seaway and pound through the hull. In terms of stability, it is a poor substitute for carrying additional ballast in the keel, where it lowers the center of gravity more effectively. If you are seriously interested in a boat with internal ballast, I would recommend that you discuss with a designer the effect of removing the internal ballast, including correction of any negative consequences of modifying the keel.

External bolted-on keels are generally lead, though some may be steel. The proper keel shape is cast and then bolted into a reinforced floor structure on the bottom of the hull. The keel bolt nuts should be snugged down and double nutted over large washers or backing plates. The standard, referred to as "Nevin's Rule," is one square inch of sectional area (of the bolt) for each

The keel bolts, nuts, and washers are all oversize on this thirty-foot sloop. The fitting on the bottom of the bilge-pump hose is a strum box or weighted strainer.

1,500 pounds of external ballast. Two rows of bolts or offsetting bolts distribute the weight much better than a single straight row. All keel bolts should be accessible for inspection and removal, since it is not uncommon for the bolts to leak or require tightening. Inadequate bolts have been known to fail. The hull external ballast joint should be sealed with a bedding compound such as 3M's 5200, which won't crack with age or stress, since the joint flexes slightly when the boat is heeled. The keel should be faired with an epoxy putty and then sealed with an epoxy sealant. The external lead keel is advantageous in a grounding, since the keel protects the hull and the lead absorbs much of the force of the impact. Our own lead keel survived a collision with a gravel bar at full throttle with nothing more than fore-and-aft gouges on the bottom six inches of the keel. Repairs necessitated by such minor groundings usually consist of nothing more than fairing and repainting the keel at the next haul-out.

Steel keels have a lower density than a lead keel. Therefore, they require a keel of greater volume (more wetted surface) or the ballast ratio will be lower than a comparable design with a lead keel. As with a steel-hulled boat, the steel keel must be meticulously protected from rust, with epoxy sealers now commonly used. Sandblasting is usually required prior to fairing and repainting a badly pitted keel. Keel bolts and their attachment within the keel must always be closely examined for corrosion since they have a higher potential (particularly on an older, poorly maintained boat) for a catastrophic failure.

Encapsulated ballast keels are an integral part of the hull. The complete hull and keel are molded as a single piece or as two

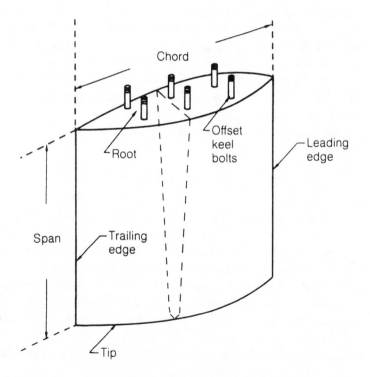

A modern external-lead fin keel. The angles of the leading and trailing edges vary dramatically with different designs.

halves (port and starboard), with a cavity for the ballast. This is filled with lead shot, concrete, iron or steel pieces, or an iron or lead casting. Any matrix ballast (iron pigs, lead shot, scrap, or the like) must be bedded in concrete or, better yet, in resin or bitumen with absolutely NO voids. The top of the ballast should be glassed or epoxied over with no air space. This is particularly important if iron ballast is used because it could expand and crack the keel if it rusted. Encapsulated ballast cannot be lost unless the bottom of the keel is scraped off in a grounding. To provide maximum protection, keel bolts should be sunk through reinforced floors into the ballast. Unlike external keels, leakage from these bolts should not be a problem. The major drawback with the encapsulated keel is its susceptibility to damage. Even a gentle grounding may require a haul-out and fiberglass work. Because of the possibility of extensive seawater intrusion into the ballast and/or glass laminate, repairs should always be made as soon as possible. To provide minimal protection, a lead or bronze shoe should be installed on the bottom and lower leading edge of the keel.

HULLS

A hull that is inadequately stiffened or strengthened will *"oil-can"* when going to weather. This term refers to the sound that the hull makes in these conditions, like beating on an empty oilcan. It means that the hull is flexing extensively, absorbing some of the forward motion of the boat. It may, in extreme cases, distort the hull enough to create changes in helm. The stresses of the flexing will cause structural damage if the boat is sailed hard over a long period of time. In a fiberglass boat, this may result in bulkheads separating from the overhead and hull, stress cracks, and delamination.

Hulls are stiffened in a variety of ways, depending upon the basic construction materials, the size of the boat, and the design. On a fiberglass boat, stiffness can be provided by one or more of the following: fiberglass thickness, coring the hull, using integral stringers and floors, an internally secured hull liner, or fiberglass taping of bulkheads and furniture. Some of these same methods are also used with other construction materials.

Aluminum and steel hulls should always be carefully checked for rust and galvanic corrosion, particularly at welded joints and through-hull fittings.

Wooden hulls should be examined for dry rot and worm damage. Wood with serious dry rot will be soft and structureless. Mold on the inside of the hull is a warning indicator, and the wood in that area should be checked thoroughly. Joints are also more susceptible to rot and should be examined. The degree of rot can be ascertained by poking progressively duller objects into the wood, starting with an ice pick or awl. If you can stick a finger directly into the hull, you definitely have problems. The only way to treat the rot is to remove all the bad wood and a smaller area of surrounding wood that appears "good" but may be in the early stages of infection.

Worms will create holes in the wood and, like termites, destroy its structural integrity. Worms inhabit salt water and are prolific in warmer tropical waters. They usually attack the hull where the bottom paint has been scraped off or in areas that are hard to paint, such as around rudder posts and in centerboard trunks. They can attack the entire hull when the bottom paint has sloughed off most of its toxicity.

Caulking in a wooden hull should be checked and a number of fasteners pulled to check for corrosion. Are there old paint layers that may need stripping? Is the hull fair? Check to see if the bow and stern overhangs sag. This is called "hogging" and is usually the result of improper cradling during storage. It is difficult or impossible to correct. Does the deck bulge at any of the chainplates? This is caused by too much tension on the rigging or by improperly constructed chainplates. Again, it is difficult to repair.

Fiberglass hulls should be examined for fairness. The fiberglass mat or core should not show through the gelcoat. This is usually cosmetic, but indicates poor attention to quality construction. Bulges, hollows, or bulkheads visible as "hard spots" on the outside of the hull may be the result of poor construction, an accident, or a poor repair. Check for crazing and cracking of the gelcoat. This is often a minor defect, but it requires further investigation if it is near stress points, such as a chainplate, the hull deck joint, or a through-hull fitting. Examine the hull for voids and delamination, and if cored, check for water intrusion or rot. Surveyors inspect for these problems by tapping with a hammer and using a moisture meter. In a few instances, the surveyor may drill inspection holes and take core samples.

The most serious concern for buyers of fiberglass boats is blistering. Contaminants such as dirt, solvents, and uncured resin can initiate blisters. They may also start forming at voids, at delaminations and stress cracks, at the boundary layers of laminates, and at the laminate gelcoat boundary. Risk factors include warm water, long immersion in water, use of orthophthalic or fire retardant resins, and poor quality control of materials or application. The standard cure for an existing boat is to grind, peel, or sandblast, dry the hull thoroughly, fill and fair, and finish with an epoxy coating. Preventive measures on a new boat include good quality control during layup and use of epoxy coatings, thicker gelcoats, isophthalic resins and gelcoats, and/or Vinylester barrier and gelcoats.

All hulls should have a strong stand-out *rub rail* with a stainless steel, heavy rubber, or bronze cap. The plastic rub rail typically used on some of the cheaper production boats will last only a couple of seasons and offers little protection for the hull.

Through-hull fittings are the weakest point in the hull. They probably result in more boat sinkings than all other causes combined. The best number of through-hulls is the fewest possible. A quality installation puts the fitting flush with the hull. This

An example of a good rub rail. A teak strip trimmed with stainless, below another stainless half-round that covers the hull-deck joint.

reduces hull friction and turbulence, as well as slightly reducing the chances of damage to the fitting. ALL through-hulls that will be below the waterline when the boat is at anchor or sailing hard on either tack should be backed by a sea cock or a good ball valve. Unfortunately, this is rarely done. We had to add ball valves to the cockpit drain and exhaust through-hulls on our boat. Gate valves, which look like garden faucets, are an invitation to disaster. It is difficult to tell when they are completely closed, they jam, they are easily damaged, and they are not always made of a marine grade bronze. Hoses that attach to any type of valve on the inside of the hull should be double-hose clamped. On used boats, always check the through-hull fittings for signs of corrosion, such as pitting. A good through-hull fitting should easily withstand a light tap from a ball-peen hammer.

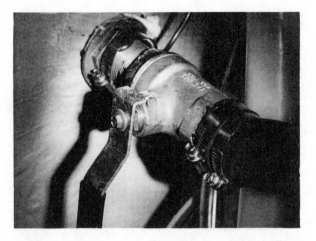

This ball valve is in the off position. Note the double-hose clamps and the copper wire bonding the through-hull to the other underwater metals.

DECKS

On fiberglass boats, the *hull deck joint* should be an overlapping flange, sealed with a flexible bedding compound such as polysulfide or 3M's 5200. It should be through-bolted every five to nine inches (³⁄₈" bolts preferred) with fiberglass taping of the entire joint. Highly stressed areas such as the stemhead and chain plates should be further reinforced.

The deck should not be springy, which is a sign of improper construction or a rotten wood core. Inspect for voids and delamination. Investigate gelcoat crazing in highly stressed areas, such as the mast step, cleats, the traveler, and chainplates. *Through-deck fittings* should be sealed and have backing plates. A standard practice is to use plywood inside the core under stressed areas to prevent compression of the core.

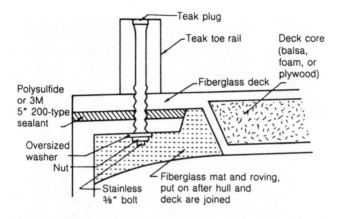

The proper construction of a hull deck joint on a boat intended for heavy-weather or offshore sailing

Nonskid can be a sheeting (such as Treadmaster), a pattern molded into the gelcoat, or an abrasive in paint. It must provide secure footing when the deck is wet or severely angled. It should be used extensively on every surface where an individual will walk or crawl. *Teak decks* make an excellent and attractive nonskid surface. In traditional construction, teak decks were laid on bedding compound and all the fasteners were bunged. In a new technique that avoids the use of screws, the teak is laid in sheets on an adhesive bedding compound. Unfortunately, teak is expensive, adds considerable weight above the waterline, gets hot to the touch in the sun, acts as a passive heat sink, is more difficult to maintain, and significantly increases the possibility of deck leaks if fastened with screws.

The *foredeck* should be large enough to work on, with few items to stub toes or catch sheets. *Side decks* should permit the easy fore-and-aft movement of crew and gear such as sail bags. *Toe rails* or *bulwarks* make the deck a much more secure and safe place to work. Toe rails should be deep to be effective and should be through-bolted (normally this is the same bolt that

An applied nonskid sheeting has been used extensively on the decks of this forty-foot sloop. The inner genoa track has been recessed, making it less of a toe-stubber.

also joins the deck and hull). Although they increase windage and topside weight, bulwarks make the decks drier and provide additional buoyancy, at least until the bow is buried by a large wave.

Lifelines should be double, with the top line well above knee height. Larger boats should have gates in the lifelines to permit easy side-deck access without having to slack the entire lifeline

This foredeck provides a good clean platform for sail handling.

system. *Stanchions* should be at least one inch in diameter and fastened to heavy, through-bolted bases with backing plates. *Stern (pushpits) and bow pulpits* should be similarly fastened. The bow pulpit should include eyes for halyards and should comfortably and safely hold a crew member working at the forestay.

Check the side-deck access yourself. This is often very poor, even on boats up to forty feet.

CABIN TRUNKS AND PILOTHOUSES

Visibility forward from the cockpit and the helm is critical. It depends upon your height, the cockpit layout, and the height of the sail clews and cabin trunk. Towering cabin trunks or pilothouses that obstruct visibility are difficult to correct without major structural changes. I find that two seat cushions work best on our boat to give me good visibility forward (I'm 5'8").

The moderate bulwarks on this boat provide more security for the crew, but increase windage and weight above the waterline. The teak decks are attractive and provide excellent footing, but increase cost and maintenance.

The cabin trunk must be a *workable area* for reefing, leading running rigging, stowing equipment, and carrying a dinghy on deck.

Handholds should be plentiful and accessible from the cockpit to the foredeck. All handholds should be through-bolted.

Hatches should be well scuppered and have gaskets. Liberal use of strategically placed hatches, such as over berths and the galley, greatly improves ventilation. Ideally, hatches should open in four directions, but those that open fore and aft are still superior to the typical hatch that only opens forward. Foredeck hatches should be large enough for passing sail bags to the deck. Hinges and latches should be of substantial construction to prevent the loss of a hatch in a storm.

Through-bolted stanchion base. The eyes provide a convenient tiedown. Note the set screws for easy removal of the stanchion post.

The pilothouse and cabin trunk are fairly well proportioned on this heavy cruising boat. Visibility around the pilothouse will be difficult when sailing. With storm shutters for heavy weather, this would make a comfortable coastal cruiser in the northern latitudes.

Skylights are beautiful, provide good athwartship ventilation, allow light into a dark cabin, and may be the only place to stand in a small boat. However, they are vulnerable to damage, take up valuable deck space, and are a constant maintenance headache and source of leaks.

Ports and *windows* must be heavily framed and sealed with a silicone sealant. Safety glass or Lexan is typically used. Opening ports greatly improve ventilation. Large window areas are very dangerous in storms or offshore and should be fitted with emergency storm shutters.

Pilothouses raise additional issues. Will the pilothouse interfere with sail handling and trimming, access to the side decks,

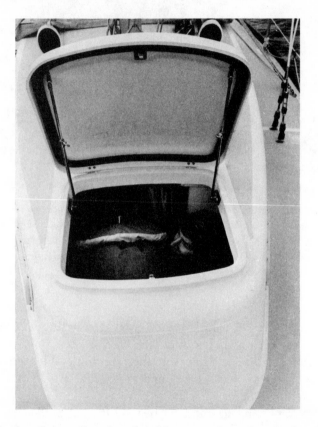

This forehatch is well gasketed and has a good overlapping lip. It is large enough to move sails easily in and out of the forecastle.

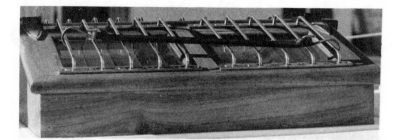

This skylight has reduced potential for leaks since it uses only four large panes. The stainless guards show a respect for the power of flailing booms and blocks.

or going forward? Will it significantly raise the center of gravity or increase windage? A major advantage of the pilothouse is that it allows an inside steering station. How complicated is the linkup with the cockpit steering, engine gauges, and controls? How good is visibility ahead, abeam, and astern? Consider what the extra steering station would add to cost.

COCKPIT LAYOUTS

Is the cockpit the right *size*? It should comfortably hold the usual crew for sailing in various conditions, as well as for an evening of conversation or for meals. If two people normally sail the boat, don't worry whether the cockpit will be comfortable for the eight people who go out with you once a year. If you intend to sail offshore or in heavy weather, you should have a small cockpit to minimize the effect of a boarding sea that fills the cockpit. *Cockpit drains* should empty a filled cockpit quickly. Two 2-inch diameter drains are a good start for

Large windows such as these provide a great view and additional light on a gloomy day. However, because the windows can be easily smashed, storm shutters must be used during heavy weather.

a small cockpit, with more drainage for larger ones. Cutaway transoms, transom doors, and dinghy self-bailers are other ways to drain a cockpit. Watch out for screens, strainers, and sharp bends in the outlet hoses, which will reduce the flow.

The cockpit should have a substantial *coaming/splash rail* to keep out boarding seas. It should be comfortable as a seat when steering from the rail and should be angled for good back support.

The *cockpit well* should be narrow enough to allow you to prop your feet against the opposite side when sitting to windward. This also reduces the cockpit volume. If the well is too wide, a hinged foot rest should be provided.

This winch coaming is wide enough to sit on when you need to get well out on the weather side. It also serves as a backrest for the cockpit seats and as a splash rail for water surging down the deck.

All boats should have a high sill above the cockpit sole at the *companionway*. Hatch boards must be available to raise the height of the entrance of the companionway to the level of the lowest portion of the cockpit coaming. Except in fair weather, companionway doors are never a substitute for hatchboards because they can be pushed inward by a breaking wave. Offshore boats should have a bridgedeck at least as high as the cockpit seats. This has the added benefit of increasing space below-decks. The safest, but most inconvenient, approach is to eliminate any access from the cockpit and position the companionway entrance on top of the cabin trunk.

This cockpit well is narrow enough to provide good bracing for the crews' legs when the boat heels over.

Cockpit lockers and lazaret hatches must be well sealed, scuppered, and able to be securely fastened or locked. Though rarely done, the ideal locker would be sealed off from the rest of the interior to prevent flooding of the entire boat if a hatch is lost in a storm.

The helm should be comfortable and well laid out. Other boats and the trim of your sails should be easily visible. The helm seat should be comfortable to sit on and should provide good back support. Instruments and gauges, especially the compass, should be visible without strain. Engine controls and the bilge pump handle should be easily accessible. The helm position should have the best protection possible from rain, wind, and spray. The sheets and traveler should be easily accessible so the person on the helm can make small adjustments without calling the whole crew on deck.

These doors are fine for fair-weather coastal cruising, but could be stove in during heavy weather unless backed with hatchboards.

Dodgers increase both windage and comfort. They protect the crew and helmsperson and keep spray and rain from entering the companionway. A dodger coaming, for the attachment of the bottom forward edge of the dodger, makes installation easier and creates a better water seal. Less thoughtful builders put the traveler for the mainsheet directly over the companionway or on the bridge deck in such a way that installing a dodger is almost impossible.

This companionway has a low sill and is closed off by two hatchboards, both securable with barrel bolts to prevent their loss in a knockdown. The lower hatchboards should always be in place in heavy weather.

Companionway hatches should be well scuppered and should slide into a seahood that is sealed forward and at the sides. The *traveler* and *mainsheet* should be positioned to avoid being obstacles to normal movements in the cockpit. *Nonskid* should be plentiful throughout the cockpit. Nice additional touches you might see include teak gratings on the seats or the sole, Plexiglas viewing ports in the hatchboards, a small cockpit icebox, a porthole into the galley for serving and conversation, mountings for a cockpit table, a spot for the life raft, and nooks for winch handles and other cockpit odds and ends.

The scuppering around this cockpit hatch is excellent and will drain even when the boat is heeled hard over.

STERN AND CENTER COCKPITS

While stern cockpits seem to dominate recreational sailboats, center cockpits have characteristics that more closely fit the needs of many sailors. At about forty feet LOA, it becomes reasonable to start considering the center cockpit as an alternative to the traditional aft cockpit. Below forty feet, the center cockpit design often results in excessive freeboard for the boat's length and division of the boat into two small, difficult-to-use spaces.

This cockpit is fairly well laid out. It has a T shape to accommodate a large destroyer-type wheel that permits steering from the high side. Note the bridge deck in front of the companionway.

Center cockpits are much drier in a following sea and wetter when going to windward. In addition, visibility is better when motoring and, to a lesser degree, better when sailing. Center cockpits allow a large aft-deck, handy when anchoring, docking, and sunbathing and useful for storing a dinghy. If the center cockpit has been elevated to increase accommodations below, the sail clews will have to be raised substantially to obtain the proper leads and permit good visibility. This effectively reduces the sail plan for light wind conditions. If the center cockpit has not been raised, it splits the interior accommodations into two separate sections. On smaller boats, this usually has the effect of eliminating the inside passageway between the fore-and-aft cabins or reducing it to a four- or five-foot high passageway. Larger boats (LOA in the mid-forties or longer) can usually have a passageway with full headroom.

A small offshore-type cockpit on a fiberglass version of a traditional double-ender. Two problems with the layout are immediately evident: the companionway doors and the mounting of the traveler on top of the stern pulpit. A few heavy-weather sails and this boat will be minus both pulpit and traveler.

STEERING

The primary choice on steering is between a wheel and a tiller. Daysailers, sailing dinghies, and small one-designs all use tillers. Tillers predominate up to an LOA in the mid-twenties. Then the use of wheel steering increases until forty LOA, when it becomes generally standard, except on a few older designs and character boats.

Tillers are more responsive than wheels, provide a more direct feel for the boat, and make it easy to envision the position of the rudder. The tiller can also be steered with the knees. Wheels offer more compact mechanical advantage than tillers. Tillers on large boats have to be extremely long to gain suffi-

This cockpit is very racing oriented: no cockpit splash coaming, almost nonexistent backrest, and traveler separating the helm from the genoa winches.

The cabin trunk profile is low and sleek on this new center-cockpit cutter. The winches and mainsheet traveler are located within reach of the helmsperson. Note the large aft cabin with its own hatch.

This nicely proportioned ketch has its cockpit located as far aft as possible, while still retaining an aft cabin.

A tiller is a simple and direct way to steer a sailboat.

cient leverage. As they fill the cockpit and require a huge sweep outside it, they become impractical. As a boat approaches forty feet, these problems make even the most serious tiller devotees start considering a wheel. Under thirty feet, tillers with more than adequate mechanical advantage can almost always be fitted.

Wheel steering is easier for novices to learn, probably because the boat steers like a car—turn the wheel to the right and the boat goes to the right. Even the simplest wheel steering system is more mechanically complicated than a tiller and will require more preventive maintenance. Wheel steering is more expensive than a tiller, running at least $2,000 extra.

If you select tiller steering, make sure the tiller is of adequate length to provide sufficient leverage when sailing with a heavy weather helm. The tiller should also be strong and stiff, with no excess movement between it and the rudder. If you choose wheel steering, you must have an emergency tiller that meets these standards and can be quickly and easily installed.

Unlike tillers, wheels are used with different mechanical systems, which vary greatly in complexity, sensitivity, and power. Quadrant steering and other cable systems are the most popular in modern boats. Quadrant steering is light, powerful, and sensitive if properly installed. It enables the wheel to be installed at a location somewhat remote from the rudder shaft. A variation on quadrant steering replaces the quadrant with a drive wheel. Another variation eliminates some or all of the sheaves by running the cable through a conduit. Called "pull-pull," it permits even more flexibility in the position of the wheel in relation to the rudder shaft.

Another wheel system is hydraulic steering. It is commonly used on center cockpit and inside pilothouse helms, where the linkage between the wheel and the rudder shaft is tortuous. In addition to being excellent for these remote installations, hydraulic steering is powerful and relatively simple. Unfortunately, it eliminates all "feel" (steering feedback) from the helm.

Rack and pinion and "worm gearing" are the oldest, simplest, and most failure-proof of all wheel systems. They offer little flexibility in installation, however, since they must be mounted directly over or ahead of the rudder shaft. This often means that the helmsperson must sit aft with poor protection from the weather and a limited view of the instruments. Sensitivity is less than with quadrant steering, particularly in worm installations.

While each wheel system will have its own installation and maintenance peculiarities, all wheel systems should generally meet some basic criteria. Magnetic materials that would affect the compass should not be used in any part of the system. There should be guards for all pedestal-mounted compasses and instruments. All parts of cable systems should be completely aligned and secured to prevent misalignment. The system should work smoothly and without any excess play or binding through a full swing of the rudder. One pound of pressure on the wheel should initiate movement through the rudder's full range.

Binding or sloppiness in the steering system, stalling during a turn, or excessive weather helm could be the result of other problems, such as a bad shaft bearing, a bent rudder shaft, a misaligned shaft tube, a poorly shaped rudder, or a keel that just doesn't want to turn.

IX.

SELF-SURVEY CRITERIA FOR THE RIG

After examining the keel, hull, deck, and cockpit, the rigging and sail plan are the next most important areas. After all, you are buying a SAILboat. The quality and condition of the standing rigging are determined by its design, installation, and past use and maintenance. Losing any part of the standing rigging may result in loss of the mast. Loss of the mast can result in extensive damage to the boat or even sinking.

The running rig and sail plan drive the boat. Again, their design, installation, and past use and maintenance have a direct and noticeable impact on a number of factors, including the level of physical effort required, personal and boat safety, ease and convenience of sail handling and sail adjustments, boat speed, ability to point into the wind, balance of the helm, future maintenance, and sailing enjoyment. By putting the emphasis on the "sail" in sailboat, you will find that you can sail when other sailboats are at the dock or under power.

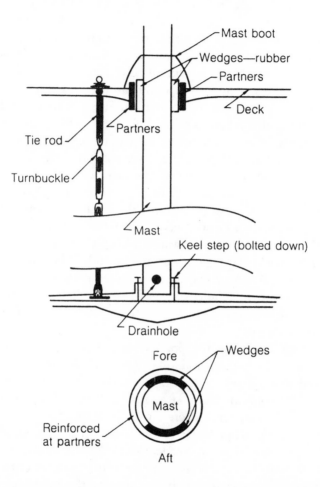

The proper installation of a keel-stepped mast. The wedges align the mast, the first step in tuning the rig. The tie-rod, which may be a rod or wire, keeps the deck around the mast from hinging upward.

STANDING RIGGING

The *keel-stepped mast* is a strong arrangement that can save the rig in a knockdown or if a shroud or spreader is lost. It usually enables the backstay to be completely slack when hauling the boat without resorting to temporary runners. It requires a crane to step and unstep the mast, may interfere with the interior arrangement of the boat, and is slightly more expensive than a deck-stepped mast. If the mast heel comes out of the mast step because of damaged rigging, the lower portion of the mast could seriously damage the interior of the boat.

Keel-stepped masts should be aligned and properly wedged at the partners (the opening where the mast passes through the deck). They should be stepped on a reinforced floor, and never directly on the keel (if you want to keep your keel). The heel should be out of the bilge water and should be bolted to a substantial step. A tie-rod should be installed parallel and close to the mast to prevent the coach roof from hinging or rising. The mast should be sealed off at the partners with a good waterproof seal and mast boot.

In contrast to keel-stepped masts, *deck-stepped masts* are much easier to put up and take down, especially if they are attached to a tabernacle (a hinged bracket that acts as a step). This is an important factor if a crane will not always be available, or if the skipper and crew intend to step the mast themselves. A deck-stepped mast should rest on a substantial step fitting that distributes the vertical thrust of the mast. The heel of the mast should be bolted to the step or pinned through a tabernacle. The coach roof in the area of the mast should be heavily reinforced and supported from below with bulkheads or other reinforcement, including a compression bar directly under the step. On a field trip with my students, we came upon the results of inadequate mast support. A mast had compressed a coach roof so much that it looked like a saucer in the area around the step.

A keel-stepped mast as it looks belowdecks. The wedging at the partners and the mast step are hidden by trim.

However stepped, the mast should be evaluated for strength, stiffness, and windage. Racers generally want a narrow mast section to minimize drag and increase the flexibility for tuning for different sails and wind conditions. For sloops, this usually requires double, triple, or even quadruple spreaders, struts, baby stays, and running backstays. While this approach definitely improves the boat's performance, it also is more complicated to set up and tune and has a much lower margin for error. Cruisers generally forgo some of the performance edge for a stronger, stiffer, less complicated, and more forgiving rig, such as the masthead Marconi rig with a single set of spreaders and an oversize mast section. Larger cruising boats may have to resort to using double spreaders and running backstays for heavy weather work. Whether the rig is for racing or cruising, a tapered mast is an advantage. Although it costs more, it re-

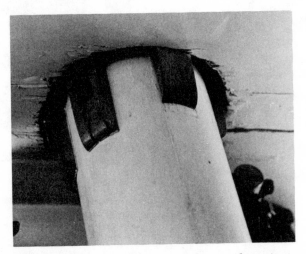

Wooden wedges have been used to align this wooden mizzenmast in the partners. Hard rubber wedges are used with aluminum masts.

duces weight aloft and windage with little corresponding reduction in strength.

Unstayed freestanding masts are usually keel stepped and tapered. While they are not taken seriously by many racers, these masts are of great interest to cruisers. They radically reduce the complexity of the rig by eliminating the stays and chainplates (and the stresses these generate), some of the winches, many feet of line, and most of the foresails.

Spreaders are a critical part of the system to keep any stayed mast in column. Aluminum spreaders are preferable to wood because they are stronger and impervious to the rot that can

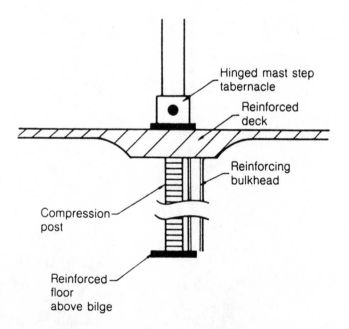

The installation of a deck-stepped mast. The reinforcement of the deck and the compression post (usually wood or stainless) prevents damage to the deck caused by the downward thrust of the mast.

A typical double-spreader rig with single outer shrouds, double lower inner shrouds, and single intermediate inner shrouds.

plague the out-of-sight, out-of-mind wooden spreader. Spreaders should have an airfoil shape to reduce windage. They must be correctly aligned to avoid premature failure and through-bolted to the mast. The tips should be wired or clamped to prevent movement on the shroud, then taped and booted or covered with baggywrinkle to prevent sail chafe.

The *mainsail boom* should be a substantial spar section, with room for all the fittings required for the running rigging, including blocks for the reefing clew lines, topping lift, outhaul, and the like. All bronze and stainless hardware used on aluminum booms and masts must be well bedded and/or mounted on plastic or rubber pads to prevent galvanic corrosion of the spar. The gooseneck that fastens the boom to the mast should be a strong universal joint with reefing tack hooks. Check for standing and sitting headroom under the boom. A low boom and mainsail with a long full hoist makes a good light-air combination, but may knock a few heads on a jibe. A boom gallows on

These aluminum spreaders have a foil shape and have been tapered toward the shrouds.

a cruising boat is a good safety and convenience feature. It provides a secure place to store the boom, will prevent injuries to the crew if the topping lift breaks, provides additional handholds, and can be used to help support an awning or dodger.

Staysail booms are found on some cutters. Their primary advantage is that they hold the foot of the staysail tight for slightly closer sheeting. A single sheet can be led to a foredeck track, making the staysail self-tending. The boom and its hardware, however, add to the cost, complexity, and weight of the boat, as well as creating a hazard for any foredeck crew within range of the boom's sweep.

A heavy-duty gooseneck. Note the large tack hook for reefing that curves to the port side.

The *shrouds* and *stays* are critical components of the stayed mast. Wire should be 1 × 19 preformed stainless of adequate diameter to ensure a large safety margin. Keep in mind that the working load of wire is only 20 percent of its ultimate breaking strength. At 60 percent of its breaking strength, wire is permanently deformed. All tangs (fittings on the mast to which shrouds are fastened) should be through-bolted and correctly aligned with the shrouds. Toggles (which create a universal joint for movement of the wire athwartships and fore and aft while maintaining correct alignment) should be on the deck end of all standing-wire rigging and on both ends of all sail-carrying stays. All wire should end in a terminal rated for marine use. Turnbuckles should be oversize and open so that the threads can be cleaned, lubricated, and inspected. There should be no excessive spaces between terminals, toggles, tangs, clevis pins, and chainplates. A backstay adjuster should be installed. These vary from a simple turnbuckle to a hydraulic pump.

A boom gallows such as this supports the boom when the mainsail isn't in use. The three slots for the boom are traditionally lined with leather.

Rod rigging, popular with racers, is seen often on cruising boats. It has several advantages. Rod of any given diameter will be stronger and have less stretch than comparably sized wire. As a result the size of shrouds and stays can be reduced, with a corresponding decrease in windage. Bonding at the terminal end of the rod is exceptionally good, and if kept properly

This wheel backstay adjuster provides a simple and fast way to tune the backstay.

aligned with toggles in both ends of the rod, it is almost failure-proof. In comparison, the most common reason for rigging failure is wire failure at or in the lower terminal. Unfortunately, rod rigging costs substantially more than wire, and it cannot be easily replaced in remote areas.

Chainplates should be securely through-bolted and fastened to reinforced structural portions of the boat, such as the hull and major bulkheads. A wider chainplate stance provides more

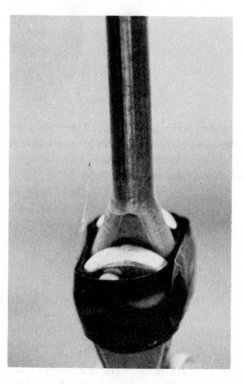

A swagged marine terminal on the lower end of a stay. This is usually where most rigging failures occur.

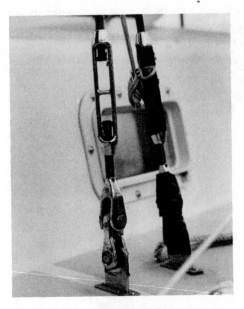

In descending order, a threaded swagged terminal, an open turnbuckle pinned with straight cotter pins, a toggle, and a chainplate. The taping on the turnbuckle to the right is to protect the genoa and sheets from rips and chafe.

support for the mast, with external hull-mounted chainplates providing the maximum. By widening the shroud stance, the rest of the standing rigging may be simplified without losing support for the mast. The farther outboard the chainplates are located, however, the less closely the jib can be sheeted in and the less high the boat can point. External chainplates are also more prone to corrosion and damage.

Stemheads should be substantial fittings, through-bolted to backing plates and reinforced at the stem. They should have at least two tack points. The best stemheads on larger boats are usually custom castings.

A chainplate through-bolted to a bulkhead

Bowsprits are used to extend the foot of the sail plan so that larger sails and more sails can be carried. This may be done on a heavy boat that needs extra working sail area for light wind conditions without having to resort to a spinnaker. It can also be used to balance the boat's helm or to increase stability by lowering the aspect ratio of the sail plan. Some designers also add bowsprits because they make a boat look more like a traditional ship, and that sells boats. Bowsprits serve secondarily as anchor platforms on which rollers can be mounted and anchors stored. In terms of weight distribution, this is a poor location to hang anchors while passage making. The really long bowsprits used to be called "widow makers" because they were such dangerous areas to work. Even with a good pulpit platform and netting, they are still nasty places to be in heavy weather. The bowsprit is also prone to damage during docking, when it can spear other boats or collide with the dock. It is a highly stressed and complicated arrangement for supporting the forestay, and

External chainplates, such as these, provide good support for the mast, but increase the angle of the sheet leads with a resulting increase in the tacking angle.

the bobstay always seems to chafe the anchor rode or twang the anchor chain.

Boomkins are used at the stern to bring the backstay farther aft and outboard so that a longer boom and larger mainsail can be fitted. Their advantages and disadvantages are similar to those of bowsprits, though on a smaller scale.

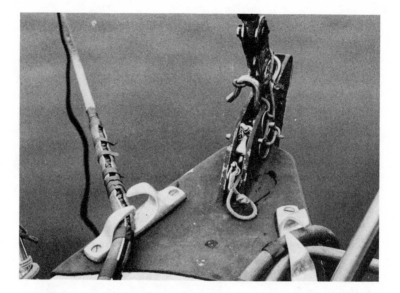

This stemhead is a custom (for the builder) aluminum casting that includes multiple tack fittings and provides for mounting of the bow chocks.

RUNNING RIGGING

Halyards can either be wire rope or low-stretch synthetic line. *Wire halyards* have very little stretch and windage. They require a rope tail and thus an expensive and difficult splice. Line stoppers/clutches cannot be used with wire, since at least three loops of wire should be passed around the winch to avoid loading the splice. Headsails of different sizes will usually require a wire head pendant. Wire halyards can also inflict nasty wounds if you're not careful.

This short bowsprit provides good security for the crew. It also houses the anchor rollers, which are close to the hull where they produce less stress on the boat and provide better weight distribution.

Low-stretch rope halyards are easier to handle and can be used with a variety of line stoppers/clutches and self-tailing winches. Low-tech polyester line stretches more and has more windage than wire. Exotic lines made of Kevlar or Spectra have stretch comparable to wire and have lower windage than standard polyester line. They are very expensive and may have a shorter working life.

Halyards may be run either inside or outside the mast. *External halyards* are commonly used on daysailers and almost exclusively by cruisers. Compared with internal halyards, they are cheaper and easier to rig, can be led away from the mast to stop "halyard chatter," and are easy to inspect and re-reeve.

Internal halyards are favored by racers and some cruisers because they offer another increment of improved performance. They reduce windage and mast-induced turbulence that inter-

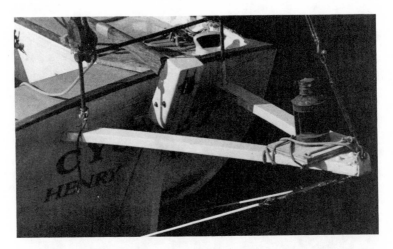

A boomkin brings the backstay aft of the hull. This permits a longer boom (more sail) and eliminates complications between the tiller and the backstay that occur with a stern hung rudder.

feres with a clean air flow to the mainsail's luff. They must be carefully installed to avoid weakening the mast and chafing on fittings that protrude into the mast column. Even with these precautions, internal halyards are more prone to chafe. They are difficult to inspect and replace and can convert a mast into a constantly clanging bell.

All *halyard leads* should be checked for fairness to be sure there is no unnecessary friction or chafing. Ideally, turning blocks mounted on the coach roof should be fastened to a collar attached directly to the mast. As a minimum, they should be bolted to large backing plates. All blocks should turn easily, have large unworn sheaves, and be strong enough for their maximum potential loads.

Sheet leads should be closely examined. If the boat has chainplates mounted inside the hull, an inboard track with a

Three internal halyards come from the exit box on this mast. Note the bad lead on the center halyard.

block on a sliding car provides the close sheeting angles that enhance windward performance. Pad eyes with snatch blocks or fixed turning blocks may also be used, but they don't permit adjustment of the sheet angle for different sails and wind speeds. All boats should have sheet leads on the rail outside of the lifelines for heavy wind work and for sailing off the wind. These leads, which will be the only ones for overlapping head-sails on boats with external chainplates, may be a track with a block on a car or a perforated aluminum toe rail to which a snatch block is attached.

Check the length of the track and the placement of pad eyes on a fore-and-aft axis. Production boats often don't have the proper leads for sails at the extremes of a possible sail inventory, such as a 180 percent genoa or a storm jib. If you are ordering or building a new boat, have the extra track and/or pad eyes put on while the boat is being constructed. It will be infinitely easier and cheaper than ripping out the interior later to fasten down and back the bolts. Two years after purchasing our boat, we found that we required a five-foot extension of our inside track forward to accommodate the correct leads for a heavy weather jib. Rather than face tearing up our boat, we compromised and installed single pad eyes on each side. All tracks, pad eyes, and deck blocks used for sheet leads should be through-bolted to backing plates. Track should be true and unwarped. Blocks should be large enough to easily withstand the maximum loads they may bear since overstressed blocks can deform or even explode, sending shrapnel across the deck.

Winches are used almost exclusively on modern boats over twenty feet to control sheets and, as boats approach the mid-twenties, to raise halyards. There should be enough winches to do the allotted jobs, but not too many, since superfluous winches translate into extra money, weight, and maintenance. Line stoppers, clam and cam cleats with thoughtful line leads, and labeling can reduce the number of winches required. These alternatives have load limits and slippage problems, however, that are not shared by directly leading a line to a winch.

Winches should be powerful enough to perform their assigned function without needing a gorilla for a grinder. Winch power is a function of the gear ratio, the drum diameter, and the length of the handle. This is referred to as the "power ratio." It should be compared for various winches to determine how easily each will work. A power ratio of 1:35 means that for every pound of effort the grinder puts into the winch, there will be a line pull of thirty-five pounds. Another way to increase the efficiency of the winch is to have a double grip on the winch handle. This permits the efficient use of both arms and shoulders. Unfortunately, higher power ratios mean slower winch speeds. To compensate for this, larger winches are made in two and three speed models. The smaller gear ratios are used for lower loads or when a faster action is desirable, and the higher ratios are used for higher loads. The standard winches furnished on production boats are generally not powerful enough except for small working sails at low wind speeds. You may need to upgrade those winches so that they are one or two sizes larger. Our sheet winches are one size larger than a comparable stock boat, and the last few feet of sheet are still hard to crank in if we are approaching the upper wind speed limit of a genoa.

Self-tailing winches are an excellent investment for the short-handed crew. They chafe the sheets slightly but permit two-handed operation without a tailer, are instantly available for increasing sheet tension, and are self-cleating. They are most advantageous for the genoa and mainsail sheet winches. If you really want to splurge, they can also be useful for reefing, halyard, and spinnaker winches when using all rope or wire with long rope tails.

Ease of winch maintenance is an important consideration since cruisers should break down, clean, and grease their

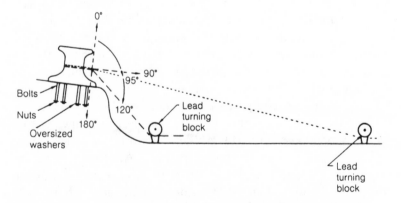

The correct installation of a winch. The line should approach the drum at an angle between 95 and 120 degrees to prevent overrides and ensure smooth operation.

A self-tailing genoa winch, well worth its price on a larger boat

winches once or twice each season. The serious racer may do this before every major race, at least for the sheet winches. This is a messy and laborious task that isn't made any easier by the complexity of some winch designs. From a maintenance viewpoint, winch bases that must be completely unbolted from the boat to clean the bearings, gears, and shafts are probably the worst type since they encourage you (and me) to defer maintenance. All winches must be through-bolted with backing plates or oversize washers.

Winches should be mounted to prevent line overrides. This means that lines should approach the winch at 95 to 120 degrees, with 0 degrees being an imaginary line parallel to the winch drum and pointing directly upward. *Winch cleats* must be through-bolted using a backing plate or large washers, and must be aligned on a 315- to 135-degree axis with the winch at 360 degrees.

Correct alignment of a cleat and winch

Mainsheets are subject to larger loads as boat size increases, with a corresponding increase in the power required in the block and tackle. Mainsails under approximately two hundred square feet can be easily handled with a three- or four-part tackle. A winch becomes advisable with larger mainsails, unless the main is going to be handled dinghy style, when a six- or even eight-part tackle might be used. This size tackle, however, is less practical because much of the mechanical advantage is lost to friction and the system becomes increasingly slow. Boom failure is much less of a potential problem if the mainsheet is led to the end of the boom, where it can counter the tremendous forces that develop on the mainsail's leach. Mid-boom sheets should be led to two or three bails in order to distribute the load on the boom.

Travelers provide versatility for the mainsail both in light and heavy weather. As the mainsail gets larger than approximately two hundred square feet, a block-and-tackle arrangement may be necessary to move the mainsheet car back and forth along its track.

Vangs, outhauls, downhauls, topping lifts, preventers, and spinnaker/whisker poles all have a place on racing boats and the well-equipped cruising boat.

All *lines* should be checked for size and condition. Double-braided lines are easier to hold on to, more chafe resistant, and slightly stronger than three-strand line. On the other hand, they have a tendency to knot up and tangle, are harder to splice, and are more expensive. Rope-running rigging is either dacron or one of the other prestretched or low-stretch synthetics. Generally, a ⅜-inch line is the smallest that can comfort-

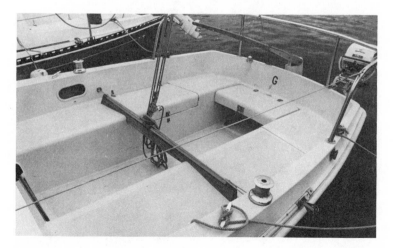

This traveler is aligned correctly to the boom, but will be a real shin banger.

ably be handled under load, although a ⁵⁄₁₆-inch line can be used for lightly loaded and less frequently used lines. Whenever possible, lines should be spliced rather than knotted since splices are both stronger and neater.

Running rigging and sail handling gear should be carefully evaluated in terms of the type of sailing, the size and layout of the deck, the size of the sail plan, and the size and strength of the crew. For instance, a single-hander may want to run every line into the cockpit, but this may cause needless spaghetti and complexity for a boat sailed with a large crew. You should always consider what sail handling will be like in a blow, since difficulty increases geometrically with increases in wind speed. This is when you are sure to find problems in your system.

Regardless of the running rigging arrangement, all lines should be logically grouped, labeled, and/or color coded. There

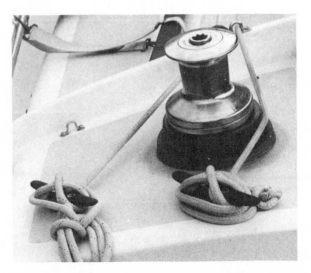

Spinnaker and genoa halyards led back to a single winch beside the main companionway

should be cleats for all the tails and, if you want to be really organized, line bags or pockets for the tails of lines that are constantly adjusted. Remember that more deck hardware means more holes and more potential leaks. Consider how the running rigging layout impacts other activities or equipment, such as mounting a dodger, walking on deck without constantly tripping on lines, stowing a dinghy, and so forth.

Main boom topping lifts are a requirement for all but the smallest of boats. The topping lift tail should be led to the same spot where the reefing lines and halyards are handled.

The lines that control the mainsail (halyard, outhaul, topping lift, and reefing clew and tack lines) can either be led to the base of the mast or back to the cockpit. They should, however, be kept together if one person is to raise, reef, and drop the main efficiently. Even if everything is led to the cockpit, someone must still go forward to tie up the excess sail after a reef or to furl when the sail is dropped.

Genoa and spinnaker halyards are typically led to the base of the mast on a standard production boat layout. By leading them aft to the cockpit, however, they can be more effectively and safely controlled. In most cases, this can be done fairly easily since only the halyards have to be brought back. Boats intending to do serious spinnaker flying may elect to bring the foreguy and topping lifts back into the cockpit, too. Short-handed cruisers with hanked sails should seriously consider rigging and leading a jib or genoa downhaul back to the cockpit so that foresails can be doused without going to the foredeck.

SAILS

Sails are the boat's horsepower. High-quality, well-cut sails will have a long, useful life if properly cared for and will improve boat speed, balance, and windward ability. High quality doesn't have to mean high price. Even though most of the well-known national lofts make excellent sails, you are paying at least in part for their reputation, advertising, and sailmakers who are world-class sailors. Excellent sails are also available from less well-known lofts, often at lower prices. Before you shop, make a list of specifications for the construction of your sails so that you know you are comparing similar products.

Sails offered by some builders and dealers in "sail away" packages may be generic sails from a large discount loft. Construction often matches the price: cheap material; less attention to reinforcement panels and chafe protection; very little handwork; reduced sail area because of a small or nonexistent mainsail roach or a short hoist or foot; and failure to include reef points, cunninghams, or leach lines.

Generally, you will be ahead in money, maintenance, resale, and performance if you select your sails personally instead of accepting a standard package. Give extra consideration to local sail lofts or sailmakers. You should get better custom design and service, as well as better local resale for your boat, if they have a decent reputation. The local sailmaker can come to your boat to take the proper measurements and discuss sheet leads and use of each sail. If there is a problem, you have the opportunity for face-to-face discussion, and repairs can be made easily and quickly, keeping your sailing "down time" to a minimum. While it may be tempting to split your sail inventory among several lofts because of price, problems with repairs, or some other reason, keep your inventory to as few sailmakers as possible. This creates better relations with your sailmaker and will enhance the resale value of your boat. If you are considering a used boat, take its sails to a sailmaker for a professional evaluation of their condition and any repairs needed. The sailmaker's evaluation is particularly important for a used boat with a large sail inventory since the sails can represent a substantial proportion of the value of the boat.

When evaluating the sail inventory of a used boat or deciding on an inventory for a new boat, your decisions are affected by cost, performance, durability, and the type of sailing you intend to do. Very competitive racers who are not seriously constrained by finances will have a large sail inventory, with each sail optimizing performance within a relatively narrow wind range. Construction and weight of materials used are matched to the performance and wind range of each sail.

Cruisers and low-budget racers usually have a smaller sail inventory. This may be because of the cost of sails, limited stowage room, or the reluctance of many "relaxed" sailors to change sails every time the wind varies a few knots. These sails must have a long life span and a low probability of failure. They also must accommodate a wide wind range. Sails carried at or beyond their upper wind range should not be permanently damaged by distortion or be blown out. Consequently, sails for these sailors are usually built sturdier. Cloth used is one or two weights heavier than an optimum racing sail. More reinforcement is included at the head, tack, clew, and reef points. Grommets are larger, reinforced, and hand worked. Extra chafe protection is provided at slides and lugs, tack, and clew rings. All heavy weather sails are triple stitched.

Assuming you can't purchase your entire inventory at once, your first set of sails is usually referred to as the "working sails." These sails will be used over a wide range of wind conditions and will probably suffer the most wear and tear. In some cases, these may be the only sails the boat will ever have. The most important criteria in selecting them should be the average wind conditions you expect in a typical sailing season.

The usual modern masthead sloop will have two working sails, a main and a jib. Flexibility in the sail plan for this rig comes primarily from choosing the foresails and free-flying sails such as spinnakers. If you expect very light winds in the summer sailing season, you will need a somewhat larger working jib (small overlapping genoa) to give the boat decent performance. This would mean a genoa in the 115 to 130 percent range, depending upon how conservative you are. These percentages

A mainsail with three sets of reef points, enabling the main to function over a wide range of wind speeds

refer to a percentage of "J," which is the distance from the mast to the forestay as measured on the deck. This is measured on the sail as a line intersecting the clew and meeting the luff at a right angle. The 115 to 130 genoa won't be a hot performer in extremely light winds but will at least move the boat. If heavily constructed, it will also carry the boat into the middle wind ranges and, without the main, might be useful running in the 25-plus knot range. We find that our own heavy 130 is a great running sail without the main until about 35 knots.

When you get tired of languishing in light summer winds or being passed by boats with more sail area, your next sail might be the biggest genoa that will fit on your boat or that is permitted by your racing rules. Now you can really start enjoying fair-weather sailing, especially if your boat has a low displacement-length ratio.

As you gain experience, better outfit your boat, and extend your sailing season and trip lengths, your chances of being caught in heavier weather will increase. Now you should consider a heavy weather, long hoist jib of from 80 to 100 percent. This sail would keep the racer competitive in higher winds and would enable the cruiser to beat off a lee shore or punch to windward to a safe port. It would be cut flat, triple stitched, and practically bulletproof.

The next sail might be a full spinnaker or cruising spinnaker (generic name for this sail is gennaker) for light to moderate downwind sailing. If going offshore, a storm jib (storm staysail for a cutter or staysail sloop) and a storm trysail (loose footed sail set behind the mast) would be added. If racing, your next acquisitions might be to fill the gaps between your No. 1 genoa, your working jib, and your heavy weather jib. Examine your own situation closely when planning a sail inventory and its order of acquisition. Talk to other sailors and your sailmaker, but focus on your own sailing area, sailing season, weather patterns, and type of boat.

You have three basic choices for headsails: luff foil head-stays, roller-furling, or hanks. Racers invariably opt for the *luff foil headstay*, in which an aluminum or plastic extrusion fits over the forestay. Sails are raised by feeding a luff tape into a slot in the extrusion. The luff foil reduces windage and turbulence, thus improving performance, particularly to windward. With double slots, quick sail changes are possible without ever going "bald." The problem for cruisers is that the luff is not attached to the forestay when raising and dropping the sail. Two or three crew are required to raise sail easily or to drop it in heavy conditions.

Roller-furling headsails are very popular with cruisers and are now frequently seen on shorthanded racing boats. Rolling up on their luff, they eliminate bagging and unbagging of sails, some belowdeck sail storage, and trips to the foredeck in foul weather. Roller-furling sails are, however, more expensive, more complex to install and maintain, and more apt to fail. They also increase weight aloft and windage. Another potential problem is that the sail may not unfurl, or worse, the sail won't roll up. To properly furl, the sail should be cut fairly flat and with a high clew, both of which are detrimental for light air sailing. While the negatives can be discouraging, it may be more fun to be SAILING with a less efficient roller-furling sail than motoring with a sail plan you find too difficult to handle.

Roller-furling is not the same as roller-reefing. With roller-furling, the sail is either completely set or completely furled. With *roller-reefing*, the sail and the gear are designed for a partial furl. The gear is at least one size larger than recommended for roller-furling, and the sails are specially constructed to take the stress of reefing and to reduce the performance loss that occurs when the sail is reefed. The advantages of roller-reefing include a smaller sail inventory and fewer headsail changes. A disadvantage is that even with special construction the sail gets fuller as it is reefed. This causes more heel and less drive, just the opposite of what is desirable in heavy conditions. In light conditions, the roller-reefing sail won't perform as well because of its heavier construction. Roller-reefing sails should not be reefed more than about 20 percent to retain reasonable performance. As a result, trying to use one headsail for 1 to 50 knots will be unsatisfactory. An inventory of two to three headsails will still be needed for cruising. The luff of a roller-reefing sail feeds into a foil, so changing to a smaller sail as conditions deteriorate can be difficult for a shorthanded crew, making it critical to change down early.

Hanked sails are the cheapest, most trouble free, and easiest to repair of any of the sail attachment systems. A major advantage for shorthanded cruisers is that hanked sails are easier to change, because the luff is secured to the forestay. This makes them easier to control, roll, and fold. With a jib downhaul, the poor person's roller-furling, the headsail can be dropped and secured on the foredeck without leaving the cockpit. Hanked sails can have slab/jiffy reefing with a reef tack and clew similar to a mainsail. As with roller-reefing, it is not advisable to reef a headsail by more than about 20 percent, and reef points should be restricted to 140 percent or smaller genoas. Construction of the full sail should match the requirements of the smaller reefed size, although this will hurt performance in lighter winds.

A favorite rig of mine for offshore or serious coastal cruising is a cutter or staysail sloop with a 130 to 140 percent roller-reefing genoa. The inner stay (with quick release) would set either a hanked heavy weather or storm staysail.

Another decision is between *low-* or *high-cut* clews. Low-cut deck-sweepers offer better performance but make for exciting sailing in tight quarters and heavy traffic, unless you have a leeward spotter. Low-cut deck-sweepers also have a tendency to scoop up water in heavy seas. This puts tremendous strains on the rigging and can damage sails.

Mainsails can be built with a hollow leach and no battens, with a roach and short battens, or with maximum roach and full battens. The hollow leach and battenless mainsail is often

A typical roller-furling genoa rolled up on the forestay when not in use. The dark material is a narrow strip on the foot and luff that protects the sail from UV light. The drum at the bottom holds the line used to furl the sail.

selected for offshore cruising. Its advantages are that it reefs well and requires less maintenance. Because of its flat cut and lack of roach, however, it will suffer in light winds. A mainsail with short battens and a small roach will provide more power in light to moderate air. Power can be further enhanced by having the sail made with a full cut and a shelf. Full battens permit a maximum roach, limited only by the backstay. They reduce flogging and enable the sail to be easily stowed on the boom using lazy jacks or one of the new systems like the Dutchman. Full battens are, however, more costly to make, require more maintenance, and can jam against the mast or in the shrouds when raised or lowered off the wind.

The most popular system for reefing mainsails is *slab* or *jiffy reefing* (the terms are synonymous). The sail is partially lowered, new reefing tack and clew points are secured, and excess sail in the foot is folded and tied to the boom with reefing pendants. Daysailers don't usually have reef points, but a single deep reef would make the boat more versatile and easier to handle in heavy weather. On a keel boat, two **deep** reefs in the main are usually adequate for coastal sailing. Offshore boats require a third reef and/or a storm trysail. The advantages of slab reefing are that it is simple, easy to maintain, inexpensive, and can make the main very flat for maximum performance in heavy air. It requires some effort to put the reef in, but if properly planned and installed the effort isn't excessive. For a short-handed cruising boat, all the mainsail controls, including the reefing system, should either be led to the starboard base of the mast or to the cockpit.

Another option for mainsails is *roller-furling/reefing*. The furling gear may be mounted behind the mast or within a mast cavity. Behind-the-mast units are less expensive, have less windage and weight, and can be retrofitted to existing masts. The disadvantages are that they put the mast under tremendous compression, make it difficult to get adequate luff tension, and develop turbulence in the gap between the sail and the mast.

In-the-mast units keep the compression forces within the mast and eliminate luff sag. They increase windage and weight aloft because of the large mast section. The main can also jam in the slot when furling or unfurling the sail unless the mast is designed with an open cavity for the furling gear. Furling/reefing mainsails cannot use battens and should be cut flat and with a hollow leach. This seriously compromises their light wind performance. When reefing, they tend to get fuller rather than flatter, which is just the opposite of what is desirable in heavy conditions.

In an older form of roller-furling/reefing, the main rolls around the boom. The pros and cons are similar to the system that furls on the luff. To get a proper reef, extra material should be pulled out of the leach and tension maintained on the halyard while turning the furling handle, making it almost a two-person job. Several new versions of this old system, with the main furling around a rod inside the boom, are now on the market. At least one of these claims that battens can be used with their system. The special boom and gear (and sometimes a new mainsail) for these newer systems makes them very expensive compared to slab reefing.

X.

SELF-SURVEY CRITERIA FOR THE ENGINE AND ELECTRICAL SYSTEMS

You can spend a surprising amount of time installing, maintaining, and fixing any of the mechanical or electrical systems on a boat. As a boat grows larger and more complex, the time and costs involved can be overwhelming. Keep your mechanical and electrical systems simple, and you will spend more time sailing.

MARINE ENGINES

The major considerations in selecting a marine engine are horsepower, installation, reliability, and safety. Choices have to be made between outboard and inboard, gasoline and diesel. Your decision will have an impact on your enjoyment of the boat, the purchase and long-term ownership costs, and the amount of time you spend working on the engine.

Selecting *engine size* involves several compromises. Factors to consider include the amount of room available for the installation, the negative effect of engine weight on sailing performance, the amount of power desired in adverse conditions, and long-term maintenance costs. Engines that are smaller in weight and horsepower can generally be bought for less, are easier and cheaper to maintain, have better fuel economy, and have less impact on weight distribution. The disadvantage will be performance under power. The underpowered sailboat may not reach hull speed in calm conditions and may barely make way into a heavy sea. With slightly more power, the boat may reach hull speed in calm conditions but may be significantly slowed when punching into a heavy sea. You must decide how much boat speed you expect or need in both calm and heavy weather conditions, bearing in mind that a sailboat under sail is much more comfortable and performs better in heavy weather than a motoring sailboat.

The true sailboat auxiliary engine is designed to power in and out of anchorages or when conditions are so light that significant progress cannot be made under sail alone. One and a half horsepower per one thousand pounds (three horsepower per ton) is a good rule of thumb for the power requirements of a sailboat using an inboard engine. This ratio should enable the boat to move at hull speed through flat water at "cruising throttle." Speed will, of course, be affected by how easily the boat is driven (hull form, displacement, and clean bottom), the condition of the engine and shaft bearings, the efficiency of the gear box or drive system, and the type of propeller. A larger horsepower-to-weight ratio is more appropriate for outboard powered sailboats since the higher RPM outboard is less effective in propelling the boat and should be throttled down to avoid prematurely wearing out the engine.

Gasoline outboard motors are the simplest solution to the power requirements of many sailboats. They are available in two-cycle or four-cycle engines and in a variety of sizes. Some are made as sailing versions with long shafts, low gear ratios, large three-bladed props, remote controls, alternators, and zinc anode protection. Outboards are normally used on sailing dinghies, daysailers, micro-cruisers, and small racing sailboats when inboard engines are impractical because of their weight, size, and cost. As a sailboat approaches twenty-six to twenty-eight feet and about five thousand pounds displacement, outboards become both less popular and less effective.

The advantages of outboards are low initial cost, portability, simplicity of installation, and the wide availability of mechanics and parts. A disadvantage is that outboards have shorter life spans because of their high RPMs, lighter construction, exposure to the weather and sea, and their high potential for galvanic corrosion and theft. Outboards have a short cruising range because of their high fuel consumption and their normal reliance on a few portable fuel tanks. Outboard engines are noisy and their alternators, often unreliable because of their exposed location, generate only trickle amounts of current. Unless the outboard is installed in an inboard motor well, its performance in reverse and in turns is poor, although turning both the motor and tiller (if you're coordinated enough) can compensate. When the boat pitches in rough seas, the prop may come out of the water and race, damaging the engine. Racing also causes the engine to be largely ineffectual in rough weather. Transom-mounted motors can also be flooded and killed by a following sea.

Until the mid-1970's, *gasoline inboard engines* were usually installed on sailboats. The Atomic Four, designed in 1949 as a marine engine, was the gas engine most commonly used. Thousands of them are still chugging away in older boats. The marketplace today heavily discounts boats with gas engines, with price reductions of $5,000 or more not uncommon. Some sellers with gas-powered boats cannot even get a call in response to their ads. This prejudice against gas engines can be a tremendous bonus for the buyer willing to accept a gas-powered boat, as more boats will be available for selection at better prices from sometimes desperate sellers. Many of these engines are, however, nearing the end of their life expectancy. If a gas engine needs anything beyond a minor rebuild, it is usually better to repower with a diesel. Repowering should also include a new fuel tank, fuel lines and filters, exhaust, and perhaps a new engine bed. If you like Universal diesels, you're in luck, because they can be installed to directly replace Atomic gas engines. The possibility of a repower should be considered in your initial offer on the boat and in future ownership cost.

Gas inboards run smoother and quieter than diesels because they usually have more cylinders and they operate at higher RPMs. They also have a cleaner exhaust. They are easy to hand crank or start on a low battery because of their low compression ratios. The most serious disadvantage of gas is its volatility due to a very low flash point. Gasoline fumes are also heavier than air and consequently, the bilge and engine compartments must be well ventilated to prevent a dangerous buildup of fumes. Sniffing the bilge should be a routine chore, particularly before starting the engine. Gasoline leaks should be treated as imminent emergencies. On a pragmatic note, few gas-powered sailboats have burned or blown up and the same cautions must be observed for propane, now the fuel of choice for cooking. Other disadvantages of gas engines include their high fuel consumption and the vulnerability of the ignition systems to moisture and corrosion.

Inboard marine diesel engines are installed in almost 100 percent of new boats and in repowering most boats with gas engines. Marine diesels include adaptations of utility and industrial engines, marine conversions of car and truck engines, and a few engines designed specifically for the marine environment. Many of the new high RPM engines are light, small, efficient, and smooth running. On the other hand, the older designed, low RPM, high torque diesels are still often selected as the ultimate in reliability and longevity. When buying a used boat, check to make sure that mechanics and parts are still available for that engine, since some very fine engine manufacturers have had their parts distribution and repair organizations fall apart.

A significant advantage of the diesel engine is its high fuel efficiency, both because diesel fuel has more BTUs than gasoline and because the diesel engine is able to extract a higher percentage of the available energy. Diesel fuel also has a high flash point, giving it a low explosive potential under normal temperatures and pressures. Diesel engines are more heavily constructed than gas engines to accommodate high compression ratios. They also don't have the moisture and corrosion prone ignition systems of gas inboards.

The diesel engine has several negatives, although they can be accommodated with a little patience. Diesels are very sensitive to dirt, air, and water in the fuel and require a high quality fuel filter system without leaks. In addition, algae likes to grow in the bottom of the fuel tank at the fuel-water interface, making it important to keep the tank clean and to frequently add a biocide. Fuel problems can result in erratic engine operation, the engine dying at inopportune times (when entering locks or trying to dock), and possible damage to injector pumps, injector nozzles, and pistons. Over approximately 15 horsepower, a diesel engine is almost impossible to hand crank (and they are difficult under 15). Thus, most diesels are dependent on an electric starting system, with its potential for shorts, corrosion, and failure, just like the gas engine. In addition, most large diesels use glow plugs, which require large, fully charged batteries. Even with glow plugs, a diesel can be hard to start in cold weather. Below 50° F., it is advantageous to use multiweight oil, and special fuel treatment is required below about 20° F. to prevent fuel gelling. Diesels also require frequent oil changes because of the high sulfur content of diesel fuel. Finally, their high compression ratios and fewer cylinders make them noisy and rough running.

A water separator fuel filter such as this is worth its weight in gold on a diesel engine. The clear bowl permits easy inspection for dirt and water, which can be drained from the petcock on the bottom.

For new or used inboard engines and used outboards, have a qualified mechanic survey *engine installation,* as well as the engine's general condition. Since engine installations on the average sailboat are often inadequate, this process can save you considerable grief and money if you decide to purchase. Before you hire the mechanic, check out the installation yourself to determine whether it meets your minimum requirements. The following criteria should assist you in your self-survey of outboard and inboard engine installations.

Outboard engine self-survey criteria

If transom-mounted, the bracket should swing up to keep the motor clear of the water when sailing. It should swing down when motoring to keep the exhaust, cooling water intake, and propeller well underwater. The deeper the propeller, the less chance it will come out of the water as the boat pitches in a seaway. As the motor head is also lowered, however, there is an increased risk of flooding the motor with seawater from a following wave. The *motor mount* should be through-bolted with backing plates. The motor should be tightly secured to the bracket and equipped with a safety chain or line. The mounting should be backed up with a lock to keep the clamps from vibrating loose and to reduce the risk of theft. Motors mounted in *wells* forward of the rudder are more efficient in turning and in reverse. They are also less apt to come out of the water and race when the boat is pitching in a heavy sea. The motor well must be adequately ventilated and the idle exhaust routed outside the well.

If the boat doesn't have built-in fuel tanks, provision should be made for an overboard *vented locker* where the outboard tanks can be secured. On larger sailboats, topmounted or remote *controls* are almost a necessity for operating the motor. Built-in *alternators* are convenient, but they are subject to rapid deterioration because of their location, and they rarely satisfy anything except the lightest electrical loads.

On any used motor, particularly one operated in salt water, check for a damaged prop, water in the transmission oil, and corrosion of the underwater portion of the motor. Motors immersed in salt water for extended periods must have a zinc anode to protect against galvanic corrosion.

Inboard engine self-survey criteria

(Criteria in bold type are essential for gasoline engine installations to avoid an explosion.)

All fittings and lines in the fuel system should be double-hose clamped, if possible, **leak-free,** and **protected from chafe.** Avoid long lengths of unsupported fuel lines. Fuel lines should be flexible hose, not tubing. All parts of the fuel or ignition system should be accessible for inspection and repair, particularly **fuel shutoffs, fuel pumps, fuel filters, carburetors, spark arresters,** bleed screws, injectors, spark plugs, ignition wires, distributor caps and rotors, coils, condensers, points and timing marks. **Fuel cutoffs must be available at the fuel tank and at the engine.** The fuel fill pipe should be secured to a waterproof deck plate/cap, and the pipe should have at least a 1¼-inch inner diameter. **The deck plate must be located so that escaping vapors are vented overboard. The fill plate, the fuel tank, and the engine must be electrically bonded for static electricity and lightning. The fuel tank must be tightly secured for the worst possible movement of the boat, and all large tanks must be baffled and/or divided into several smaller tanks. All fittings—including return fuel lines and vents—must be from the top of the tank. The vent tube should be an inner diameter of ⁹⁄₁₆-inch and must be vented overboard in a high loop to a vent that will not be submerged when sailing. Gasoline engines must have a Coast Guard-approved** *spark arrester* **on each carburetor.**

The engine compartment must be adequately *ventilated,* **both naturally and by a blower. At least one air intake duct must be installed below the level of the carburetor air intake.**

The power blower's exhaust intake must be below the level of the carburetor air intake at the lowest point in the bilge that is free of water. The blower itself must be mounted well above any possible splashing bilge water and must exhaust overboard.

The engine should be well secured on a sturdy *engine bed* of wood, steel, or aluminum. On a wooden boat, the bed should straddle four or more frames and floors. The fastening of the bed to the boat and the engine to the bed should be checked for adequacy. Flexible engine mounts are desirable on diesels to reduce vibration and noise. Adjustments for engine shaft alignment should be accessible at each engine mount or pad.

There should be a *drip or oil pan* under the engine. The engine should be painted and look clean and presentable, with little rust. Check for water leaks (indicated by salt deposits, if the engine has been run in salt water) and for fuel and oil leaks.

Pulley belts should not be cracked, ragged, or worn. Check for rubber dust, a sign that the pulleys are out of alignment. Check belt deflection. Belts should not be overly tight or slack. A half inch of deflection is a standard measure for correct tension. All belts should be easily accessible for changing.

The *exhaust system* **MUST BE ABSOLUTELY TIGHT** from the engine to the overboard discharge. All fittings must be sealed and double-hose clamped. The overboard exhaust hose must be looped high above the waterline through an anti-siphon elbow, then attached to a sea cock or ball valve, where it exhausts through the hull. All *water hoses* should be in good condition, have a fair run, and not leak. Access to the water pump for removal and replacement of the impeller should be good. There should be a grate on the outside of the hull at the water intake, a sea cock on the water intake through-hull, a water strainer before the engine, and double-hose clamps on all fittings. There should also be a drain on the engine for winterizing.

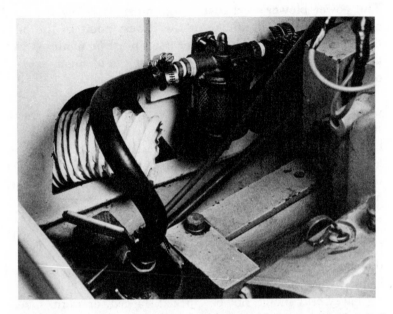

The start of the engine's cooling system should always include a ball valve or sea cock on the through-hull fitting and a water strainer. The bowl on this strainer is clear, so it can be inspected. Note the double-hose clamps.

The *engine compartment* should be insulated for heat and noise. Lead foam is the standard material for this type of insulation. Access should be good for checking and changing the engine and transmission *oil*, and the oil filter. Oil changes are much easier with a built-in oil sump and/or pump. An engine oil analysis by a lab may be a useful indicator of the internal condition of a used engine.

The *engine/transmission coupling* should be accessible for inspection and alignment. A flexible coupling is preferable on rough running diesels (most one- to three-cylinder ones) and

The access to this engine is excellent, compared with most sailboat installations, although the port and forward sides are a little difficult to work on. This particular engine is installed directly over the center of the keel (good weight distribution) in the main saloon.

on long propeller shafts to reduce stresses on the engine, transmission, and shaft bearings. The *stuffing box* (where the propeller shaft passes through the hull) should be accessible for inspection and to tighten the packing nuts. The hose covering the stuffing box and the shaft tube should be in good condition and double-clamped. The *cutlass bearing* (through which the shaft passes through the hull after exiting the stuffing box) should be checked for wear.

The *propeller* should be checked for nicks and corrosion. Folding, feathering, and variable pitch props should be in good working order. There should be some means of locking the propeller shaft to keep the propeller from freewheeling when under sail. Check the condition of the zinc on the propeller shaft or strut. If it is providing adequate protection from electrolysis and galvanic corrosion, it should be partly eaten away between normal haul-outs.

A minimum set of *engine gauges* should include tachometer, temperature, ampere-charging rate, and oil pressure. Alarms for the cooling water temperature and the oil pressure are valuable additions.

ELECTRICAL SYSTEMS

Water, particularly salt water, and electrical systems don't get along well. Some sailors have taken drastic measures to avoid problems, such as banning electricity from their boats or deep-sixing the offending gadgets. With a good installation and consistent maintenance, however, you can take advantage of the many practical uses of electricity on a boat and have a system with high reliability. To save time and money during maintenance and modifications, a wiring diagram should be obtained from the builder or developed section by section as work is performed on the system. The diagram can also be an invaluable tool in diagnosing electrical problems.

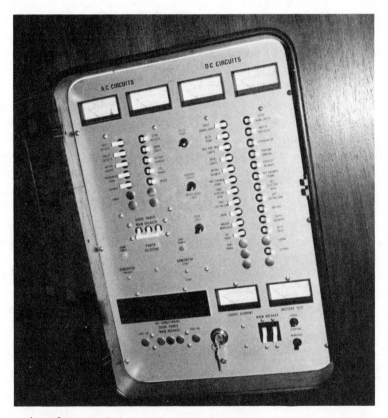

A sophisticated electrical panel for both the 12- and 110-volt systems on a large sailboat

All *wiring* should be color coded, protected from chafe or excessive vibration, and kept out of damp or wet areas such as the bilge. Electrical equipment and connections should be clean and corrosion-free. To protect against equipment damage or fire, all electrical equipment should be wired into a fuse or circuit breaker panel located in a dry part of the boat. Many builders fail to comprehend that a panel under the companionway sill is NOT in a dry spot.

Two *batteries* are recommended for boats that require electric starting, one for the engine and one for the lights and accessory equipment. Marine deep-cycle batteries are preferable. A built-in charge indicator (voltmeter) is handy to determine battery condition. Both batteries should be connected to a four-position vapor-proof switch. They should be located close to the engine so there is a short electrical lead to the starting motor, and they should be insulated from the engine's heat. Battery boxes must be acid-proof, well vented, and provide security for the batteries in a 360-degree rollover. They should be clean, corrosion-free, and topped off with distilled water. Check the batteries with a hydrometer if there is any doubt about their condition.

If *shore power* (110 volts) is wired into the boat, it must be completely separate from the boat's 12-volt system. Stray 110 voltage can cause electrolysis, damage 12-volt equipment, or give a crew member a fatal shock. All 110-volt systems must be grounded and should incorporate a Ground Fault Circuit Interrupter (GFCI), which can save your life if you accidentally become an electrical ground.

Through-hull fittings, mast, engine, fuel tank, keel bolts, propeller shaft, chainplates, and the zinc should all be electrically bonded with No. 8 wire to protect against galvanic corrosion and provide a rudimentary lightning ground.

Interior lights should be the minimum size necessary for their function and should be well distributed throughout the boat. Fluorescent lights draw much less current and should be considered for the large lights in the main cabin or for use in the head. They can, however, interfere with radar and electronic navigation equipment. Red night lights and rheostats are worthwhile power and night-vision savers.

Deck lights are useful for deck work after dark. Unfortunately, these lights are exposed to the weather, to vibration fatigue, and to direct breakage from sails, halyards, or radar reflectors. Spreader lights are popular but are more susceptible to damage than mast-mounted lights.

Running lights should be as bright (given power limitations) and visible as possible. Mountings on the bow and stern pulpits are much more visible than hull or deck mountings and are less likely to be damaged by collision with an out-of-control dock. Running lights must be well sealed. All sockets and bulbs on a used boat should be checked for corrosion. Masthead navigation lights provide superior visibility when offshore or navigating near large ships. They can be combined with an emergency strobe and/or anchor light.

After completing your review of the electrical system, consider whether the average daily draw of the boat's lights, appliances, and gadgets will exceed the capacity of the alternator, the battery, or your personal tolerance for motoring to the extent necessary to keep the electrical system running.

XI.

SELF-SURVEY CRITERIA FOR BELOWDECKS

On any boat with accommodations, it is the belowdecks systems that make living aboard (even if only for a weekend) possible. With proper design, installation and maintenance, they can be serviceable and even provide some conveniences and comforts. With poor design, installation or maintenance, they can be an aggravation and can create some interesting character-building situations. In some instances, belowdecks problems can increase the risk of damage to the boat or even personal injury.

Keep in mind when assessing any of these systems that your needs in this area are highly dependent upon how the boat will be used and the size and type of boat that you ultimately select. For example, the daysailer may only need a bucket for a head, while the marina live-aboard may require a sophisticated sewage treatment system. The weekender on a small pocket cruiser can easily adjust to using a small, single-burner alcohol or kerosene stove, while the serious coastal cruiser on a thirty- to forty-foot boat may find that only a large diesel stove and oven will meet cooking and auxiliary heat requirements.

VENTILATION

Every boat should have extensive ventilation. Too much ventilation is rare except in below-freezing weather. In hot weather, adequate ventilation vents heat out of the boat and brings in cool air. At any temperature, good ventilation helps eliminate the all-pervasive dampness of the marine environment and the moisture created by breathing, cooking, and heating in a closed space. Good air turnover is also important to prevent oxygen depletion and pollutant buildup from unvented or poorly functioning stoves and heaters.

A traditional bronze port with a keeper chain (to hold it open) and dogs (to fasten it watertight)

To facilitate ventilation, boats should have a number of opening hatches, opening ports, and cowl vents. *Cowl vents* should generally be installed on dorade boxes or with water traps, so that rain and seawater will be prevented from coming below. Vents or cowls in both the bow and the stern greatly improve air circulation since the natural flow of air on a boat is from the stern to the bow. Provision should be made for complete sealing and securing of all hatches, ports, vents, and cowls in heavy weather.

Inside the boat, air should be allowed to circulate freely within all the cabins and storage spaces. There should be vent holes and louvers in all drawers, doors, bins, and lockers. When a boat is closed up for any length of time, it is important to open all the drawers, doors, hatches, and icebox lids to ensure good air circulation. Signs of poor air circulation and ventilation include stale, musty air, mold, drawers and doors that stick, condensation, and rot. Poor ventilation is death to a wooden boat.

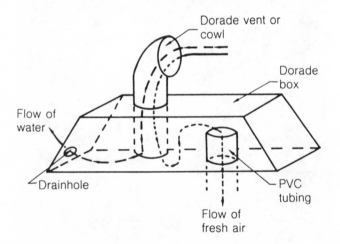

The dorade box (or water trap) lets fresh air in and keeps water out (if properly built) in all except the most severe conditions.

A cowl vent mounted on a dorade box

MARINE HEADS

Waste discharge is regulated at the federal level, as well as by some state and local jurisdictions. The following is a brief summary of several options currently available. Compliance with applicable law should be checked when you consider any particular marine head system.

The traditional *cedar bucket* (or its modern counterpart in plastic) is probably the only practical alternative for a small boat. Its advantages are minimal cost, ease of installation, maintenance-free simplicity, and no through-hull fittings. Its major disadvantage is its low capacity, and emptying it several times a day may be distasteful.

A *Porta Potti* is a self-contained, no-discharge system. After learning that this was the alternative used by our local Coast Guard commandant in 1977, we installed a $100 Porta Potti on our boat and used it almost trouble-free for five years. Porta Potti advantages are low initial cost, simplicity, reliability, ease of installation, and no through-hull fittings. Disadvantages include low capacity (usually three to six gallons), the difficulty of finding a dumping station (marinas aren't enthusiastic about

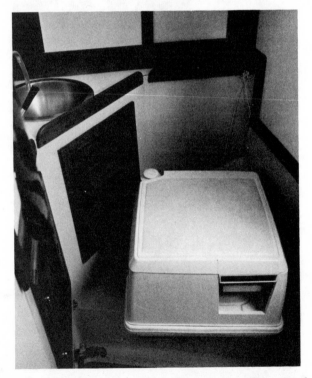

The completely self-contained Porta Potti is one of the simplest and cheapest solutions (with the exception of a bucket) to marine sanitation.

dumping in their toilets), the distastefulness of emptying them, and possible odors.

A *standard marine head with a "Y" valve* to either a holding tank or a through-hull for discharge offshore is a common installation. A deck pipe to the holding tank should also be included for pumping out at a shore station. Advantages include a larger capacity holding tank, a much less onerous emptying process, and the flexibility for direct discharge when offshore or in an allowed discharge area. The disadvantages are that it is a more costly and complicated system to install and maintain; extra space is taken up by the holding tank; there are holding-tank odors; and there is the risk of a leak or rupture in the holding tank or a line. This is the preferred option for many owners of larger boats.

Another alternative is a *standard marine head with a Coast Guard approved sewage treatment system,* routed to a through-hull for discharge. Its advantage is the ability to discharge effluent in allowed areas without holding it for later pump-out or disposal at a discharge station. Disadvantages include a complicated installation, large space requirements, odors, potential electrolysis problems, and the risk of a system failure. This system also involves higher cost, electrical demand, and maintenance. It is probably the least attractive alternative for most sailors, but in some jurisdictions it may be the only viable one.

All marine heads with overboard discharge systems should loop the discharge line high above the waterline through an antisiphon elbow. This is to prevent back-siphoning of water into the head, which can sink the boat. Heads, buckets, and Porta Pottis should also be securely fastened down to avoid coming loose in a knockdown or at extreme angles of heel.

Whatever system you select, please respect the shellfish and your neighboring boats and don't discharge in any marinas or small harbors with a slow water changeover.

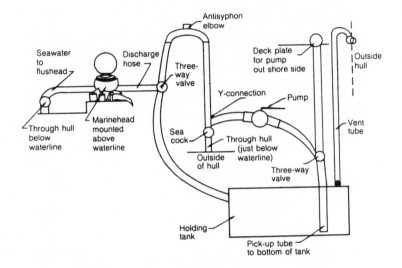

A schematic diagram of the installation of a marine head that provides flexibility for sailing in areas with differing discharge requirements. With this type of installation one can pump directly overboard or into a holding tank. The holding tank can be emptied either by pump-out at a shore installation or by pumping overboard.

WATER SYSTEMS

A good rule of thumb for required *water capacity* for all purposes is one gallon per day per person. This assumes a conscientious effort to conserve. Water requirements can be reduced by using seawater for everything but drinking and the final rinse after a sponge bath or seawater shower and by supplying a large part of your liquid intake with canned drinks. If you keep track of water consumption for a few trips, you can develop a consumption figure that fits your sailing style.

The water supply should be divided into two or more *tanks.* An easy and inexpensive way to do this on a boat with one main tank is to carry enough jerry jugs of water to serve as both the extra and the emergency supply. Permanent tanks should be baffled with inspection ports for each section and should be securely fastened within the boat. The tanks should be vented inside the boat with 9/16-inch hose looped high under the deck. The freshwater deck fill plate should be sealed tight against salt-water intrusion.

Pressure water systems are convenient at the dock when water is in almost unlimited supply but can lead to use of an extravagant amount of water at sea. They make it particularly easy for guests to drain your tanks. If a pressure system is installed, there should be at least one manual freshwater pump in case the pressure system goes on the fritz. The best solution is to have a completely parallel manual system that can be used when you leave the dock. Foot pumps greatly increase the convenience of a manual system, and if recessed, they can avoid being toe stubbers. Saltwater taps are another way to reduce reliance on fresh water, and if the tap is below the waterline, no pump is necessary.

Sinks should be deep and installed near the centerline. They should discharge slightly above the waterline. Showers should not drain directly into the bilge but should be routed to a sump and then pumped overboard. The head sink can drain into the same sump, thereby eliminating another through-hull fitting.

STOVES AND HEATERS

The type of fuel is the most important factor in selecting a stove or heater since it directly affects safety, cost, efficiency, and ease of use. After the fuel has been selected, the quality of the equipment and installation are important considerations.

Wood is cheap, readily available, and adds very little moisture to the interior of the cabin. Woodburning stoves are also inexpensive and require little maintenance other than cleaning. The disadvantages of using wood include the bulkiness of the fuel, the constant attention required to stoke the fire, the lack of control over the heat output, and the mess from ashes and soot both inside and outside the boat.

Coal, with many similarities to wood, can usually be used in the same stove. In contrast to wood, coal is less bulky for storage, has a higher heat output, and is messier before and after being burned. Since fewer homes and businesses now burn coal, it may also be hard to locate.

Alcohol is probably the most common fuel used on small boats in the United States. A large variety of stoves, ovens, and heaters are available. Nonpressurized alcohol stoves, which are much safer than the older pressurized type, are also now made. The advantages of alcohol include a clean flame when burning and a moderate flash point. Its disadvantages are its high price, the difficulty in finding it in bulk outside the United States, a lingering sweet smell, and creation of a substantial amount of water vapor as it burns. In addition, alcohol has only about half the BTUs of other fuels. Consequently, it takes much longer for heating and cooking.

Propane and *butane* are now very popular on larger boats. Depending upon the amount of care you are willing to devote to the installation and maintenance of a propane or butane system and the degree of risk you are willing to accept, either may be a viable option. The advantages are a high heat output, ease of operation (no priming is required), infinite heat adjustment from simmer to high, and a clean flame. Propane is also widely available, although a metric pigtail is needed outside the United States to fill the tanks. The complexity of the installa-tion is a disadvantage. Also, the risk of an explosion from a fuel leak is high since both propane and butane are heavier than air and will settle in the bilge like gasoline fumes.

For safety, propane and butane tanks should be well secured

in a sealed locker with an overboard vent and located close to the stove or heater. The tanks and fittings should be corrosion-free. An electrically operated solenoid valve should be installed with its switch and an on/off warning light located near the stove. A pressure gauge should be installed after the valve for leak detection. The fuel line should be a single, continuous, high pressure, propane-approved hose with approved fittings, padded and supported at frequent intervals. A bilge blower approved for flammable gases should be installed with its intake at the lowest part of the bilge and its exhaust outside the boat. Always sniff the bilge for gas and run the blower before using the stove. When the stove will sit idle, turn off the solenoid valve before turning off the burner to burn all the fuel from the line.

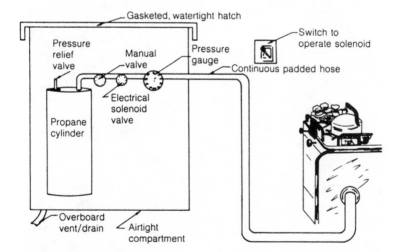

A schematic diagram of a propane installation. Properly installed and maintained, a propane stove is a joy, but carelessness can turn it into a floating time bomb.

Compressed natural gas has similar characteristics to propane or butane, except that it is lighter than air and therefore creates less risk of an accidental explosion. It is bulkier than propane or butane and may be more difficult to find.

Diesel has always been very popular in the Pacific Northwest and Alaska, particularly on fishing boats. The fuel is readily available worldwide, and if diesel-powered, the boat only requires one type of fuel. Diesel is relatively cheap and has a high BTU rating and high flash point (making it less likely to explode or catch on fire). It can also be used with a wide range of burners. Unless it is burned correctly, however, diesel can be a dirty and sooty fuel. Diesel stoves also tend to be bulky and heavy, and cooking on them in the summer or in tropical climates can be insufferably hot.

Typical installation of a propane tank in an overboard vented locker. The solenoid valve is on the left.

Kerosene was traditionally the fuel of world cruisers, although pressurized gas is now more popular. Kerosene has a high BTU content and flash point and is generally available worldwide. The Primus/Optimus burners used in most of the kerosene stoves and heaters are generally interchangeable and are also available worldwide. The disadvantages of kerosene include a smoky flame if the burner isn't clean or properly preheated and a difficult-to-adjust flame (hot or hotter). Also, each burner has to be primed before each lighting.

Gasoline should never be used to cook or heat on board a boat. It has a very low flash point and is heavier than air. In

This kerosene stove has good sea rails and pot holders. Its cast-iron top takes the chill out of the air if the cover plates are left in during cooking.

the correct mix with air, a tablespoon of gasoline can have the explosive power of several sticks of dynamite.

At colder latitudes, *stoves* with tops that resemble old-time cookstoves are useful. When the iron or steel top heats up during cooking, it can put out enough heat on a cool summer morning or evening to make lighting the fireplace or heater unnecessary. Since boat cooking is often very simple, an *oven* may not be necessary for your boat. A pressure cooker, stove-top oven, or Dutch oven will often save the space and expense of the full stove-oven combination.

When surveying the installation of any stove or oven, several criteria should be considered. The stove top should have sea rails and pot holders. If the stove or oven is gimbaled, it should be heavily counterweighted and have a lock to keep it from swinging. There should be a crash bar in front of the oven to keep the cook and crew from being thrown directly onto a hot surface. Areas behind the stove or oven should be accessible during cooking without risking a burn. Curtains should not hang over the stove or oven. The stove or oven should be securely fastened and bolted so that it will stay in place during a knockdown or rollover. Burners with automatic flame shutoffs and oven doors with safety latches are preferable.

When selecting a *heater* for your boat, consider the latitude and season in which you will be sailing, your personal warmth level, and the total amount of time you are likely to use it. For occasional use, small fireplaces, wood stoves, or single burner pressurized heaters are probably the best choice. For higher and longer heat requirements, diesel stoves or propane, kerosene, or diesel forced-air furnaces are probably a better choice. Live-aboards in northern climates and winter sailors should probably select two separate heaters, at least one of which is not dependent upon electricity (12 volts or 110 volts) to operate.

All heaters should be installed so that the crew can't be thrown against them and burned. Convection heaters should be positioned as low and aft as possible for good heat distribu-

This three-burner propane stove and oven is very cleanly installed. The bar in front of the stove protects the cook from being thrown against the stove and burned.

tion. Never use an unvented nonelectric heater in the boat without a number of hatches and ports open to vent the fumes.

Stoves, ovens, and heaters should all meet several minimum installation criteria. The fuel should always have a remote cutoff. The stove, oven, or heater should be insulated as much as is practical from adjacent flammable materials. Any insulation used should be covered by stainless steel. Stacks should be tall enough for a proper draft and should be capped with a Charley Noble (keeps the rain and spray out of the stack while letting the smoke out). The stack should not be near any flammable materials, and it should be insulated where it passes through the deck. Lastly, fully-charged fire extinguishers should be located close to each of these appliances.

A bulkhead-mounted, pressure kerosene convection heater

ICEBOXES AND REFRIGERATORS

An *icebox* is the simplest and cheapest approach to keeping food cold. It also has the advantage of being almost maintenance-free. The obvious difficulty with ice is its limited longevity. Once the ice has melted at sea, you won't be able to cool perishables or drinks until you can replenish your supply. This can be a constant hassle for the live-aboard, particularly in a hot climate. When offshore, most sailors with iceboxes learn to adjust to the fact that the "cold" will only last one to two weeks.

While coastal cruisers can usually find ice at marinas, lugging it to the boat may not be a favorite task. Iceboxes cannot maintain even temperatures as well as a refrigeration system, and they have no freezing capability.

The primary advantage of marine *refrigerators and freezers* is that they do not require ice to stay cold. They offer consistent "cold," subject only to the reliability of the system and the availability of fuel. They are significantly more expensive to buy, install, and maintain than an icebox. When not plugged into shore power, the engine must be run a minimum amount each day to keep the refrigerator and/or freezer at the proper temperature. The amount of engine time required will depend upon outside air temperatures, use and size of the refrigerator, amount of insulation, and efficiency of the compressor. A range of one to four hours per day is not atypical. "Cold" is acquired at the expense of fuel and your tolerance for engine noise, smell, and vibration.

An icebox for extended cruising should be able to hold seventy to one hundred pounds (approximately eight to twelve gallons) or more of ice and still have sufficient room for all the perishable stores. Our icebox, with only slightly above-average insulation, will hold 80 to 110 pounds of ice, plus perishable food. This typically lasts two weeks, generally permitting us to be independent of ice machines when coastal cruising.

Both iceboxes and refrigerators should have drains leading to sumps that can be pumped overboard. An even better solution for an icebox is a pickup tube to its bottom that is routed into the galley freshwater pump through a valve. The ice-melt water can then be used as a supplement to the freshwater supply (for other than drinking).

For maximum efficiency, an icebox, refrigerator, or freezer should open from the top and be insulated with four inches of foam, including the lid. Lids should be secured with hinges and hasps so they will not fly around. Be wary of iceboxes located where the top will receive direct sun, such as near a companionway. Small cockpit iceboxes are a nice convenience, but they must be sealed off from the rest of the boat or, like a good cockpit locker, be secured and have gaskets and deep scuppers.

ACCOMMODATIONS AND INTERIORS

When evaluating the interior and the accommodation plan, you must consider the boat in two states: level with little or no motion, and under way with heeling and pitching motions. A sailboat that is used principally at the dock and in fair weather doesn't need the interior of a blue-water sea boat. The most important criterion will be whether the boat is functional when not in motion. In contrast, the interior of a sailboat intended for offshore and heavy-weather sailing must meet much more stringent requirements. A stylish interior that looks great when viewed at the dock or in the security of a cradle at a boat show may be dysfunctional, unlivable, or even dangerous in a heavy sea. When sailing hard, the interior shouldn't be a place that you dread entering, with bilge water slopping over the sole, your library and gear strewn about, water taps leaking a steady stream, berths that resemble wet coffins, or passageways that require suction cups for transit. The following criteria will help you assess the practicality of a boat's interior and how functional it will be at sea.

The *companionway ladder* should be easy to use and provide secure footing both going up and coming down, even if the boat is heeling or pitching. Handholds should be accessible along the entire length of the ladder. There also should be a way (for even weak individuals) to exit through a forward hatch in an emergency.

The *cabin sole* should have some type of nonskid surface, preferably one that is attractive and easy to clean. Teak and holly, used for the traditional sole, are nonskid, easy to clean, and very expensive. Teak-plywood veneers are common on newer boats. They are cheaper and fairly nonskid but don't stand up well to wear and tear. Fiberglass soles with molded nonskid patterns are even less expensive but are usually unattractive and somewhat hard to clean. Nonskid tape or matting, or a nonskid paint, may also be used. While effective, these are hard to keep clean and uncomfortable for bare feet. Rugs are the worst choice for a permanent cover, although builders often use them on new boats to cover an unfinished or unattractive sole. Rugs slide around on the sole and get wet and moldy in the marine environment. If you want the advantages of a rug (warmth, foot comfort, and sound insulation) without the disadvantages, use one only at the dock or when anchored, and air it out frequently. When the rug is rolled up, it should reveal an attractive and functional nonskid sole.

There should be a *wet locker* for foul-weather gear. It should drain into the bilge and should be located as close as possible to the main companionway to avoid dripping water through the boat.

The boat's interior should be organized so that crew members always have support against the boat's motion as they move through the interior. Living-room-size expanses are dangerous at sea since supports are much farther apart. There should be plenty of easy-to-reach, through-bolted *handholds* in the passageways, galley and head, and above the settees. Grab poles at appropriate corners can do double duty as support for the cabin roof and as handholds.

There should be plenty of *storage space* for food, extra water and fuel, clothes, tools, spare parts, fishing gear, sails, extra anchors, and other gear and equipment. One rule of sailboat storage is that you never have enough. Many boats that appear spacious inside have created that openness at the expense of lockers, bins, shelves, drawers, and other forms of usable storage. A portion of the storage should be immediately accessible,

These companionway steps need a railing. A serious injury could result from falling the six-plus feet from the sill to the cabin sole.

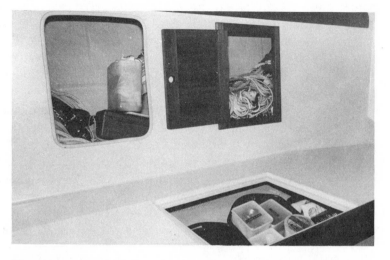

There is a great deal of storage space in this boat, both under and beside the berths.

with another part accessible without hours of searching and re-organization. Part of the storage space should be dry storage that will be reasonably watertight in severe conditions. Storage areas for heavy items should be available below the waterline.

Berths should be sufficiently high, long, and wide for comfortable sleeping without knocking your head, knees, or elbows when you move. Since few of us fit the dimensions of the "average" person, the best test of a berth is to get in it and try a few rollovers and a change of clothes drill. In particular, check the quarter berths, which should be the most comfortable berths on the boat but through poor design are often the worst. Three to four inches of open cell foam in the cushions is the accepted norm for comfort (this applies to all of the boat's cushions). If you can afford the price difference, closed cell foams are better because you can use a thinner foam. Also, they won't absorb water like the open cell foams, and they provide additional pieces of flotation in an emergency. Leeboards or leecloths should be fitted to all berths that will be used at sea so that those sleeping on the windward side won't fall to leeward and out of their berths. Many small boats convert the dinette into a double bunk. This arrangement often works only in the builder's brochure and should be checked for ease of setup, sturdiness, sleeping comfort, and impact on fore-and-aft passage through the boat. V-berths in the forecastle are another common way of adding additional berths. Unfortunately, the forecastle, a convenient spot to store sails, happens to be the most uncomfortable sleeping area in the boat when it is under way or in an exposed and rough anchorage.

The *dinette table* should be constructed heavily enough to support the weight of a crew member thrown against it. Take-

This boat is unusual in that it has two quarter berths, both spacious and comfortable.

down and folding tables should be checked carefully, since they are often flimsy.

The *chart table* should be located near the main companionway so the navigator can easily converse with the helmsperson. This also reduces the length of the trip (and the amount of water dripped) from the chart table to the cockpit position used for sights. The chart table should have a niche to store navigation instruments and tools. There should be extensive chart storage either in the table or nearby. A chart table that faces fore or aft provides a more consistent working angle on both tacks, and the navigator won't have to fight to keep level with it. This type of table works best with a wraparound bucket seat with a safety belt.

To keep things where they belong as the boat heels and pitches, every countertop, table, shelf, and storage area should have *fiddles* (raised edges) at least one inch high. Cleaning is easier if the fiddles on the dinette table and galley counters have a few narrow breaks to facilitate wiping up spilled food. Storage areas should be divided with additional fiddles and vertical panels to keep the ship's stores in place. This is especially useful if a storage area isn't fully loaded. Drawers and doors should have a positive catch that will remain closed at extreme angles of heel. All corners should be well rounded to reduce the likelihood of injury.

There should be easy *internal access* for inspection, rebedding, repair, and replacement of all instruments, through-hull fittings, and deck-mounted equipment. It is also helpful if a substantial portion of the hull is accessible for inspection and repair. All too often, good access is rare and minor repairs or replacement of equipment may mean dismantling or demolishing substantial pieces of the interior joiner work. Serious hull damage at sea may require taking an ax, saw, and crowbar to your interior to expose the damaged portion of the hull for temporary repairs. A full inner hull liner is an easy way to stiffen the hull, provides some sound and heat insulation, keeps many

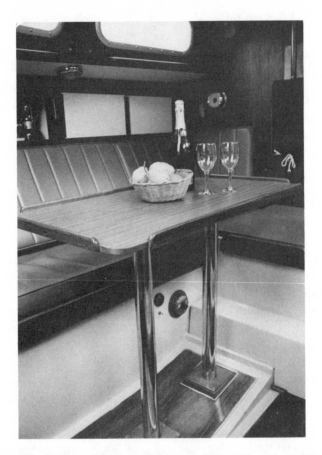

A sturdy dinette table on stainless steel legs. Note the fiddles, rounded corners, and openings for wiping food off the table. The wine, glasses, and fruit are typical of the displays set up by dealers. They won't be around after more than 10 degrees of heel.

of the leaks out of the main cabin, and provides a nice, clean interior. It also makes hull and coach-roof access very difficult and reduces the interior volume of the boat. Typical solutions to improving interior access include hinged doors, zippered or snap-out panels, and velcro closures behind instruments and major pieces of hardware.

At some point, every boat will develop deck *leaks*. But boats with better quality control will have fewer leaks since they use better sealants and take more care to bed down and seal every fitting and piece of equipment that goes through the cockpit, deck, or cabin roof. On a used boat, a conscientious owner will have fixed any leaks before they get out of control by pulling the offending fitting and rebedding it. The most common leak areas are the chainplates, stanchion bases, hatches, portholes, and windows. The best test for leaks is to close up the boat and squirt water under pressure at every through-deck fitting, the edges of hatches, and other openings. Then check below for signs of unwanted water. On a used boat, you can also look for water and rust stains beside and under fittings.

The *bilge* should have a sump to catch and hold seepage from the propeller-shaft bearing, condensation, spills, and small leaks. Many modern boats have such a shallow bilge sump that at extreme or even moderate angles of heel, the bilge water is slopped into storage areas and over the cabin sole, creating a slippery and dirty mess.

XII.

SELF-SURVEY CRITERIA FOR OTHER EQUIPMENT

BILGE PUMPS

A frightened sailor with a bucket is probably the most effective short-term answer to getting rid of unwanted water. This is, however, extremely exhausting for long periods and a pump is a better approach. The intake hose can be routed to inaccessible low spots in the bilge. A good pump can be useful for everything from small amounts of bilge seepage to major leaks from hull damage. The most efficient pumps now available are diaphragm pumps. They handle large quantities of water with a reasonable effort, will pass small debris, and are easy to repair.

Pump intake hoses should be fitted with strum boxes (weighted strainers) to block large debris from the pump and to keep the intake down in the bilge. Discharge lines should be as short as possible, with no sharp turns. They should have an inner diameter at least as large as that of the pump outlet. This helps the pump to work closer to its designed capacity. The handle of at least one main pump should be operable through a watertight gland accessible to the helm and should be secured to avoid losing it in a knockdown.

Small daysailers and dinghies should have a bucket or small bailing scoop and a sponge to get rid of water. At this boat size, a pump isn't really necessary. Slightly larger boats should carry a larger bucket and a medium-size piston pump, which is portable and inexpensive, although not very efficient. Small keel boats should have at least one medium-size diaphragm pump of at least a 15-gallon-per-minute capacity. Larger keel boats (twenty-seven feet and longer) should have at least one of the largest pumps that can be installed and a second pump as backup. The second pump can be more versatile if it is set up as a portable pump by mounting it on a spare companionway hatchboard. For an offshore boat, at least one pump should be operable from belowdecks with all hatches shut.

An emergency portable bilge pump mounted on an extra hatchboard

If space and money are available, an engine-driven highcapacity rotary pump makes a good insurance policy in the event of a major hull leak. The engine water cooling pump, the sink pumps, and the head and holding tank pumps can also be adapted for emergency use. An electric bilge pump should never be the sole pump on a boat.

This imported boat has a beautiful fourbolt bronze cleat and chock for dock lines, but the lead is not fair (straight) through the chock.

ANCHORING AND DOCKING GEAR

The bow and stern *cleats* should be substantial fittings, through-bolted, with large backing plates. Bollards (bow or stern) and samson posts (bow only) are older, traditional substitutes for docking cleats. Bollards should be installed like cleats. Samson posts may require special installation if they are modern "imitations" that are not tied into the boat's stem. Cleats amidships are useful to rig spring lines or secure dinghies.

Chocks should be large enough to accommodate the largest line aboard with chafing gear attached. The chock should have no sharp edges and any line passed through it should form a fair lead between the cleat and the mooring post or anchor. Poorly installed or manufactured chocks can destroy the best line in short order—a potential disaster.

This boat has a well-thought-through anchoring system: anchor carried on-deck in chocks ready to go, double cleats for easy handling of multiple anchor rodes or dock lines, chain pipe, and cowl vent to the chain locker.

Short *anchor pulpits* with rollers make anchor handling much easier and are excellent places to stow anchors for coastal cruising. Preferably, the pulpit should have two rollers. Each roller should be at least three times the width of the largest rode to accommodate chafing gear and should be deeply grooved with guides to prevent the rode from jumping free. All edges should be beveled and the fairleads flared to prevent chafe.

A bow *anchor locker* is an even better solution to anchor stowage. It brings the weight of the anchor lower and closer amidships, where it will affect performance less and be less likely to come adrift in heavy weather. The locker should be large enough to store at least one working anchor, plus some chain and rode. It should drain overboard and have a substantial cover with through-bolted hinges and hasps.

Although *chain lockers* typically drain into the bilge, an overboard drain is preferable. The drainage should not pass through any storage compartments. The locker should be well ventilated and have an eye or cleat for the bitter end of the rode. A metal cap typically tops off the chain pipe leading to the chain locker, although cowl vents are often used as a substitute chain pipe. The cowl vent can do double duty by letting in a good airflow. It can also be removed and sealed with a watertight screw-in cap for heavy weather. The top of a chain pipe located in an anchor locker should be raised above the locker's floor to avoid flooding of a belowdecks chain locker.

Anchor windlasses are essential for heavy anchors, all chain rodes, or those of us with weak backs. They should be made of as few dissimilar metals as possible to prevent galvanic corrosion. The windlass should have two gypsies, one for nylon and one for chain. Electric windlasses should always have a manual override. Unfortunately, windlasses are expensive, heavy and real shin bangers on a foredeck. Except on heavy boats, they usually aren't worth the costs until a boat is over thirty feet LOA.

A plough anchor stored on an anchor roller with a windlass to pull up the chain

BASIC INSTRUMENTATION AND ELECTRONICS

You can spend a great deal of money on instruments and electronics to report information on your boat's performance, the weather and sea conditions, to provide a communications link with the outside world, and even to time a soft-boiled egg. If you race seriously, good instrumentation helps keep you in the top competition. If you are a cruiser, it rates more as a convenience.

In my opinion, many instruments are unnecessary luxuries unless you have unlimited sailing dollars or are into serious racing. Electronic gadgets promoted by the boat equipment industry are expensive to buy and install. With even the best equipment and installation (often not the norm), maintenance will be a continuing problem, since salt, humidity, vibration, and other characteristics of the marine environment are very hard on electronics. Today's state of the art quickly becomes obsolete because of rapid technological changes. In addition, a heavy electronics load can quickly run down the batteries.

When you start with a new boat, put your energy and money into the essential basics of sails, rigging, hull, and engine. Add the MINIMUM necessary instrumentation and electronic gear. Restrict it to what you know how to use, can repair or afford to have repaired or replaced, and know can be handled by your batteries and alternator (or generator on large boats). When the basics have been installed, then consider adding those extra gauges, radios, and the like that may make sailing more fun and convenient. My suggestions for basic instrumentation and electronics, in order of importance, are a compass, a depth sounder, a VHF radio, and a knot meter with a log.

Buy the largest and best *compass* you can afford. The compass card should be easy to read and well dampened. Since this is a vital piece of equipment, a second compass is a good idea. Two identical compasses can be bulkhead mounted on each side of the main companionway, providing easy viewing on either tack, as well as a backup. The compass should have a guard to protect it from damage and a hood to eliminate sun glare. A good handbearing compass is an essential item on any sailboat.

Select a good *depth sounder* with the deepest feasible range. An anchor alarm is an excellent addition to any depth sounder. A properly installed in-hull mounting is adequate for navigational purposes, though it will reduce the sounder's range. A through-hull transducer provides better range but requires another hole in the hull and the transducer surface can be fouled. A flasher display is advantageous because it provides clues to the bottom consistency.

A marine band *VHF radio* provides a communications link to other boats and to the shoreside telephone system. More importantly, it gives you direct access to the Coast Guard in an emergency in most coastal waters. A 3 dB masthead antenna for the VHF radio will significantly improve reception and broadcast range.

A *knotmeter* with a log helps fine-tune sailing performance and provides the data to calculate distance traveled. Self-contained units that generate their own electricity have an advantage because they are independent of the boat's electrical system. An *RDF* (radio direction finder) is useful for homing in on a beacon and is usually self-contained, making it a good backup. Unfortunately, many RDF beacons are being discontinued in the U.S. *Loran C* is extremely accurate for coastal and inland sailing and low-end units are inexpensive. Loran errors can occur because of landmasses, during sunrise and sunset, and on the edge of zone coverage. *SatNav* is being phased out and replaced by *GPS* (Global Position Satellite). GPS is very accurate and offers worldwide twenty-four-hour position finding. It has been downgraded slightly for civilian use and does not have the repeatable accuracy of Loran. GPS units are expensive, but prices are expected to decline rapidly in the near future. Loran and GPS require a good noise filter and a voltage spike suppressor. Remember that the question isn't IF your electronics will fail, but WHEN. Make sure you have good backup equipment and basic navigation skills to get you home when your fancy navigation display goes berserk.

OTHER GEAR WORTH CONSIDERING

Even the best built sailboat requires a variety of extra equipment to ensure safety, seaworthiness, comfort, and convenience. The following represent a few of these extras that I consider important to boat safety, proper seamanship, convenience and comfort (this is where you will spend part of that 20 to 50 percent of base price for outfitting that I mentioned earlier):

■ Extra *fire extinguishers* (at least double the Coast Guard required number). Extinguishers should be mounted throughout the boat, from the cockpit to the forecastle. You have to be your own fire department at sea. Boat fires are very serious because boats are extremely flammable and burns can be life-threatening without prompt and specialized treatment.

Overboard rescue pole with strobe and drogue (in stuff sack). Drogue reduces drift of pole from victim and helps keep pole upright. Lifesling and its 150-foot tether are in bag attached to pulpit.

Extensive inventory of *flares and signaling devices* (many times the minimum number required by the Coast Guard). Flares are cheap insurance in an emergency. It is not uncommon for only half of the flares stored on a

A swim ladder attached to a split stern pulpit for easy entry and exit from the water

boat to work, and a large number and variety of signaling devices may be necessary to get attention.

- For overboard rescue, your best chance is with a *Lifesling* (training is highly recommended) and a separate *overboard pole, strobe,* and *drogue* system to mark the victim's location (skip the horseshoe; it fouls the Lifesling).

- *Radar reflector* to make you visible on the radar screen of that supertanker about to run you down.

- Two *flag halyards,* one for the radar reflector and another for courtesy and quarantine flags.

- Large *first-aid kit* that you know how to use.

Your best friend, a life jacket with attached harness. Pockets are for personal strobe, whistle, and flares.

■ *Swim ladder* so you can easily get back aboard after swimming or in an overboard emergency.

■ *Safety harness* with tether for each member of the crew. You might add a whistle, personal strobe light, and flares to each harness. Most owners will also want to run a *jack line or wire* from the cockpit to the bow for clipping on the harness tether.

■ Pair of 7 × 50 *binoculars.*

■ Minimum of two *anchors* (typical cruisers carry four or more). At least one should be a *storm anchor.* Refer to Chapman's and to the manufacturer's recommendations to determine storm anchor size. If in doubt as to the correct size, always go up one size. To sleep confidently at night in a crowded anchorage on a short scope rode, your "working anchor" should be as large as your storm anchor. The CQR Plow, the Danforth Hi-Tensil, and the Bruce are all fine modern anchors. Additional anchors to consider are a stern anchor (working anchor size), a second storm anchor, a dinghy anchor, and a grapnel. *Rode* diameters should be matched to the anchor. Again, Chapman's can be used as a guide, and if in doubt go one size larger. A ³⁄₈-inch line is the smallest that can be comfortably handled, but a ¹⁄₂-inch line is even easier to hold. The storm anchor rode should be about six hundred feet long and the working anchor rode three hundred to four hundred feet long. Use **at least** double the length of chain recommended by Chapman's and select a chain diameter one size larger to accommodate the next larger size shackle, the weakest link in your anchoring system. Experienced cruisers generally use a minimum of four to six fathoms of chain.

■ *Anchor sail.* This small sail can help hold your bow into the wind when heaving to or when in an anchorage where the current and wind are moving in different directions.

An anchor sail on the backstay of a sloop or cutter keeps the boat weathervaned into the wind at anchorages.

- *Dinghy,* to row ashore when you anchor out, to set an extra anchor, to explore, to fish, to set crab traps, and in an emergency to abandon ship. The ideal sailboat would carry both an inflatable with a small outboard motor and a hard rowing/sailing dinghy.

- Four nylon *mooring/dock lines.* At least two of these should be 150 percent of the boat's length. To go through locks, you may have to meet other minimum requirements. For example, the Ballard Locks in Seattle requires two fifty-foot lines with loops in one end.

- The longest *boat hook* that will fit on the boat, to pick up a mooring or retrieve a cushion or dinghy painter.

- Six of the largest *fenders* that will fit in your lockers and at least one *fender board.* If you can find a place for them, two of the fenders should be the large, round buoy type.

- *Boatswain's chair* for going up the mast.

- *Tiller extension* for steering from the rail.

- *Soft dodger* over the main companionway or cockpit. I feel that this is a required piece of equipment in the higher latitudes, especially for early- and late-season sailing. A dodger keeps spray and rain from below and gives the crew and helmsperson protection from the wind, spray, waves, and rain. On sunny days, it offers some shade both at anchor and under way. A soft dodger can be folded down in nice weather to increase cockpit visibility and airflow. It can be stowed below in extreme weather to reduce windage and avoid tearing and ripping. A good, soft dodger is a cheaper and more versatile alternative to a hard dodger, doghouse, or pilothouse. When evaluating a dodger, make sure it will fit under the main boom when sailing with the outhaul loose, halyard slacked, or downhaul tensioned. Visibility should be adequate, there should be good access to

A full set of covers will pay for themselves many times over in maintenance. Even the dinghy has a cover on this boat, to save the owner varnishing time.

the side decks, and the winch handles must clear it when they are turned.

- *Weather shields.* These make the cockpit much cozier when running or reaching downwind and when at anchor, particularly during the cooler months.

- *Awning* or *boom tent* to offer protection from sun and rain. This can be a simple or a custom-designed solution to weather protection. It does not, however, work very well when sailing.

- *Foul-weather gear* and high rubber boots, with layers of warm wool or synthetic clothing for off-season sailing.

- *Pressure kerosene lantern.* These put out a great deal of light (equivalent to a 200- to 250-watt bulb) and some heat, without draining the batteries.

■ *Portable shower*, for bathing on the dock or down below.

■ Good set of *tools* and *spare parts* to fix all your supposedly "trouble-free" equipment (see following section).

TOOLS AND SPARE PARTS

Every boat should carry tools and spare parts for emergency and permanent repairs. Even the highest quality and best maintained boat will occasionally need repairs away from the dock. The more complicated the boat and the more equipment there is on it, the more likely it is that repairs will be required unless the boat rarely leaves its moorage or is never sailed hard. There aren't marine service stations on every point or island, and the Coast Guard is supposed to be a rescue service, not a boat-towing and repair company. Broken gear at sea can be serious, and you should be prepared for maximum self-sufficiency, consistent with your level of sailing.

A small daysailer with an outboard motor that is used exclusively for day sails on a freshwater lake doesn't need one hundred pounds of tools and parts. It should, however, carry a few basics, such as: spark-plug wrench, screwdriver, pliers, crescent wrench, propeller cotter pins, round cotter pins for rigging, light line, wire, tape, and a set of spark plugs. At the other extreme, an offshore cruising keelboat might carry hundreds of pounds of tools and spare parts, including such "necessities" as a spare alternator, starting motor and water pump, an extra backstay, spare halyards, blocks, and so forth. A permanent workbench might even be installed to facilitate onboard repairs.

The coastal cruiser is between these two extremes. It needs to be prepared for routine maintenance under way, and for many of the same emergency repairs an offshore boat might require. Critical problems must be handled immediately. You won't always be near a boatyard when the engine quits, the mast falls down, or the hull starts leaking. Although small problems might not initially threaten the boat's integrity or your safety, they can be a serious inconvenience that can ruin a vacation cruise. Boatyards and marinas may not have the parts or skilled labor that you need, and if they do, you may have to wait in line for service during the peak sailing season. Solving your boat's problems and learning additional skills is satisfying and will be useful if you move to a larger boat or take more adventuresome trips to remote places.

In Appendix B you will find a suggested "starter" list of tools and spare parts for a coastal cruiser. The list can be modified according to your skills, the type and size of boat, and how far away from civilization you plan to be. Daysailers may also find some ideas in this list, though they will want to pare it extensively. The offshore sailor and those going overseas will find that this is a good starting point, although many more items should be added, including all spares difficult to obtain overseas or essential to a safe and enjoyable trip. Of course, any purchase of tools and spare parts will be limited by your budget and the available storage space on the boat.

XIII.

EVALUATING THE DESIGNER, BUILDER, AND DEALER/BROKER

The reputation and background of the designer and builder should be important factors in your purchase decision. Their reputations should give you a general idea of the expected performance, seaworthiness, and quality of a given boat. In addition, their reputations and past practices should suggest what you can expect in the areas of resale value, warranty service, and maintenance. You should also do some research on dealers (and brokers, if you're looking at used boats), if potential warranty work, quality of boat commissioning, and postpurchase service will be important factors in your decision.

Focus your assessment of designers, builders, and dealers on the areas mentioned below. You can obtain most of this information by talking to other sailors and reading. In addition, don't hesitate to call, write, or visit the designer, builder, and dealer. If still in business, they are usually happy to answer reasonable questions from prospective clients.

THE DESIGNER

How long has the designer been drawing commercially salable boats? What specific designs are credited to this designer? Do these designs generally match the type of boat you are considering? For example, be wary of the first fiberglass racer drawn by a designer who has always done wooden cruisers.

What is the general reputation of the designer's boats? What are some of the specific histories of boats designed by this person, such as number of hulls constructed from a specific design, racing results, or cruises undertaken?

THE BUILDER

How long has the company been building sailboats and how many has it built? How long has the designer or design team worked with this particular builder? A close relationship generally results in a better-built boat.

How long has the builder been constructing the specific boat that you are considering, and how many have been built? Was this boat ever constructed by a different builder? If so, inquire about the performance of previous versions. Check the reputation of the builder with other sailors; from anecdotal stories concerning cruises, storms, and races; and in boat evaluations and reviews in the sailing literature.

Can you go to the factory and inspect a boat under construction? This is worthwhile if you are serious about a specific boat, know what to look for, and can easily make the trip. Will the builder accommodate changes or modifications at a reasonable cost? What is the extent of the warranty on paper and in reality based on other owners' experiences? Is the builder bondable and willing to be bonded for the construction of your boat, a particular concern when so many companies are having financial difficulties.

THE DEALER/BROKER

How knowledgeable is the dealer (or broker, if that's the case) about sailing, sailboats, and the specific boats it is selling? How long has the dealer been selling sailboats, and how long has it been selling its current line of boats? Does the dealer have a yard and a service manager? What is the quality of its work on warranty, commissioning, and repairs? What do other customers say about the quality, timeliness, responsiveness, and cost of its work? Is the dealer reasonably accessible by auto and boat? If the dealer is using high pressure, be careful not to commit yourself until *you* are ready.

XIV.

MAKING THE DECISION

Now that you know more than you ever cared to know about sailboats and the many alternatives and compromises you must face in making your decision, you need a rational process to sort everything out. There are many ways to narrow your choices, but I think the following method is particularly good at making sense of a large amount of data. In part, it summarizes steps outlined in detail in earlier chapters.

PRELIMINARY STEPS

First, review the "selection prerequisites" list that you prepared when you began the process of deciding whether to buy a sailboat. Discussed in Chapter II, this outlines your anticipated utilization and financial constraints and is the starting point for your sailboat search. At this stage, you should already have a rough idea of your size requirements.

Decide what your best alternative is for gaining access to a sailboat (discussed in Chapter III). Consider crewing with friends, a sailing club, chartering, building a boat, buying a used or new boat, shared ownership, and chartering your boat to others for profit and/or tax purposes. Be tough with yourself and pick an alternative that best meets your current circumstances.

If you decide to build or buy a sailboat, make an initial decision about the type of construction material for the hull and deck: wood, ferrocement, steel, aluminum, a composite, or fiberglass (Chapter IV). Decide what type of rig or sail plan would best match your needs: cat, sloop, cutter, yawl, ketch, schooner, cat ketch or schooner, or motor sailer (Chapter V). Consider the type of underbody that would most suit your performance requirements: multihull versus monohull; centerboard, daggerboard, or keel; full keel or fin keel; spade rudder or skeg- or keel-attached rudder; and outboard or inboard rudder (Chapter VI).

Based on these decisions, develop an initial list of potential "candidate boats." You can obtain ideas for this list by attending boat shows, reading the sailing literature, visiting a wide variety of dealers and brokers, touring marinas, and talking to sailing friends. Develop a file on each candidate, incorporating relevant articles from books, and magazines and materials obtained from dealers, brokers, builders, and designers.

APPLYING PERFORMANCE CRITERIA

Next, complete the data column of the Performance Criteria Checklist for Buying a Sailboat (see Appendix C) for each boat under consideration. This information, discussed in Chapter VII, can usually be obtained from ads and brochures, articles, boat evaluations, dealers, builders, and designers. If necessary, you can do some of the calculations or at least come up with an approximation. Don't worry if you can't get data for every criterion for every boat. Some data are better than none, and as you narrow your candidates, you can pursue further research.

APPLYING SELF-SURVEY CRITERIA

Review the Self-Survey Criteria (Chapters VIII to XII) and select five to ten characteristics that are critical to meeting the original selection prerequisites you've set for your boat. Write these on the Self-Survey Criteria Checklist for Buying a Sailboat (see Appendix D). Then complete this checklist for each of your candidate boats.

Although you will have intuitively narrowed your list of candidates as you collected data, your list of boats may still be extensive. Dealing with this amount of data in any logical and analytical way is difficult because a boat that meets your standards in one area may be deficient in another.

SCORING AND RANKING

Scoring and ranking the boats is one effective way to analyze the data you have collected. Assign a weight to each criterion on the two checklists (Appendix C: Performance Criteria and Appendix D: Self-Survey Criteria) based on its value to you. For instance, if light wind performance is important to you, give the Sail Area-Displacement Ratio a weight of three. If of only average importance, assign a weight of two; if of little importance, a weight of one; and if of no importance or irrelevant to your decision, a weight of zero.

After you have assigned a value to each criterion, score each boat on how close it comes to your ideal. A one to ten scoring system works well. In the above example on light wind performance and Sail Area-Displacement Ratios, the boat with the highest ratio would get a ten and boats with lower ratios would be given appropriately lower scores. Scoring is probably the most difficult part of this process because each criterion will require a different manner of scoring, depending upon the buyer's selection requirements. For example, some-one interested in heavy displacement sailboats would assign boats with high displacement-length ratios a high score, while someone interested in ULDBs would give them a low score. In contrast, someone interested in boats with moderate displacement-length ratios would assign progressively lower scores to boats as they moved away in either direction from the moderate mid-range.

The next step is to multiply the scores you have assigned by the values for each criterion included on both checklists. Then add up all the weighted scores for each boat. Rank all the candidate boats on your list in order of their cumulative scores. The total score for each individual boat represents a composite of your needs and how a particular boat meets those needs.

Take approximately three to six of the top-ranked sailboats from your list and evaluate them in more detail. If you have done your research carefully, probably any one of these boats would meet your basic needs. This means your final decision is among boats that are comparable. The scoring and ranking pro-cess provides a benchmark to determine if you are headed in the right direction. If you are still interested in a sailboat that didn't get a high ranking, or if boats in which you haven't any serious interest ranked high, something may be wrong with your decision-making process. You may have been unrealistic in de-termining your selection prerequisites, had inadequate data, se-lected criteria that don't relate to your real needs, or weighted or scored the criteria incorrectly.

OWNER REFERENCES

To further evaluate this smaller group of top-ranked boats, you should discuss each boat with several (I recommend at least three) current or prior owners. Ask:

- What are typical boat speeds under sail upwind and downwind, in both light and heavy air?
- Does the boat respond quickly to the helm in calm conditions, heavy air, and in close quarters?
- Will the boat track with little attention to the helm, on the wind and off the wind? How much weather helm does the boat have?
- Does the boat have any tendency to broach or pitchpole when running in heavy wind?
- Do seas ever enter the cockpit when beating or running in heavy weather?
- How many degrees between close-hauled port and starboard tacks?
- At what angle of heel does the boat sail fastest and have the best helm?
- Does it sail around the anchor? Does the bow blow off during close-quarters maneuvers?
- At what wind speeds are headsail changes and reefing done? How much effort does this require?
- When pounding into a head sea, does the boat have any tendency to "oilcan"?
- How much effort does sheeting in the main- and head-sails require? Are the winches adequately powerful?
- What is the boat's performance under power? What are cruising speed and top speed into a heavy sea and wind? How does the boat turn under power? Will it back un-

der power? What is the average fuel consumption? What is the amount of engine noise and vibration?

- What has broken, been repaired, or required modification? Where does the boat leak?
- Has any warranty work been done, and was it completed satisfactorily?

Ask about any other specific concerns you have. Most owners like their boats and will usually respond positively to the general question: "How do you like your boat?" To get useful information, you must ask specific questions.

THE TEST SAIL

Should you take a test sail?—not necessarily. (Note that in some instances a deposit or charter fee may be requested before you can take the boat out). Either take a test sail on all of your top-ranked boats under similar weather and sea conditions or don't sail any of them. Otherwise, you will have information that will be difficult to compare. Ideally, you should sail each boat in light and heavy weather, and if it has overnight accommodations, take it out for at least one long weekend. If you have the patience, chartering the boats in which you are interested is an excellent way to get acquainted with them.

If you do take a test sail, I suggest that as a minimum you check these areas of the boat's performance:

- Is there excessive weather helm?
- Will the boat balance and track true with little attention to the helm?
- How many degrees between tacks when sailing hard on the wind?

- How easy is it to use the running rigging? How much physical effort is required to trim the sheets?
- Is the standing rigging tuned? Is the mast properly aligned?
- How difficult is movement on deck and belowdecks?
- Does the hull "oilcan"?
- What are top and cruising speeds under power?
- How does the boat handle under power in close quarters? Does the bow blow off severely? Will it retain steerage while backing down?
- How much noise and vibration does the engine generate?

Appendix A, Sea Trials Checklist, is the guide I currently use when helping a client with a test sail. If you cannot take an extensive test sail, the Performance Criteria, independent boat evaluations, and comments of other owners are critical, since they provide your only forecast of the boat's performance in a variety of conditions.

DOING THE SELF-SURVEY

The full Self-Survey Criteria, Chapters VIII to XII, should only be applied to your final pick or top two or three ranked boats. Appendix H, Sailboat Evaluation Checklist, is what I currently use to guide me when I perform a full boat inspection with a client. You will need an inspection mirror, flashlight, small magnet to check which metals are ferrous, tape measure, piece of #8 wire (correct minimum size for lightning ground and galvanic corrosion bonding), Swiss Army Knife, small hammer with a nonmarking head, pen and paper, hand rag, boat shoes, and work clothes. Examine every system with a fine-tooth comb. Be prepared to spend at least a day crawling in and out of lockers and other odd spots. Comments from owners or others familiar with the boat can be helpful in providing leads for follow-up, particularly on difficult-to-inspect areas.

OTHER QUESTIONS

If you still have questions or concerns that haven't been satisfactorily answered by the seller, other owners, a test sail, or your self-survey, contact the builder or designer directly. Appendix E, Summary Data Format for Buying a Sailboat, provides a suggested method for summarizing the background of the designer, the builder, and the dealer; the critical points from other evaluations; the references provided by other owners; and the results of the test sail.

PRICING

To know how much you are really paying, you should calculate a comparable price for each of your top-ranked boats. To do this, you will have to consider the cost of modifying each boat to make them all similar, though not necessarily identical. This requires adjusting the "sail-away price" of each for equipment and modification costs. For instance, if you want a kerosene stove and one of your top-ranked boats has no stove, add the cost of a new kerosene stove. Another boat might come with an alcohol stove. Subtract the resale value of the alcohol stove and add the cost of a new kerosene stove. Many modifications may be too structurally difficult or costly, and you shouldn't adjust the price to reflect them. For example, adding the cost of dorade boxes and vents to a boat is reasonable, but adding something like a bridge deck is usually such a large and costly project that you'd probably never undertake it.

Adjust the "sail-away price" by subtracting the credits and resale values associated with equipment you don't need and adding the cost of extra equipment and modifications. You will then have a realistic and comparable price for each of the top-ranked boats. At this point, you have to decide whether the price differences are worth the substantive differences in the boats and whether there is any room for you to modify the seller's asking price.

An interesting way to compare boats is by dollars per pound. To calculate this, divide the final comparable cost figure by the boat's displacement. This provides a good benchmark to test your assessment of the boats. As a general rule, quality increases with cost per pound. A boat that you thought was of high quality but is relatively inexpensive by the pound may be underpriced and an exceptional bargain. More likely, you have overestimated its quality and something in its construction justifies its low price. A boat selling for top dollar per pound is probably of very high quality. It may also, however, be overpriced due to an advertising-created, inflated reputation. Again, match the price with your own assessment of a boat's quality. Appendix F, Pricing Worksheet, provides a method for determining the comparable real costs of each boat.

To be totally realistic about cost, look at the long term. Select a period—for example, the first year of ownership, your projected length of ownership, or the period of your loan. Calculate the full estimated costs of ownership during the period selected, including the down payment, monthly payments (less tax advantages), moorage, maintenance and repairs, extra equipment, and insurance. Keep in mind that a boat needs constant care to stay in good condition and that eventually even the best-maintained systems will require total replacement. Appendix G—Long Term Costs Worksheet—provides a suggested approach for calculating long-term ownership costs.

RESALE

You should also consider the resale value of any boat you might buy. If a boat is unique, strange, one of a kind, or very expensive, it may resell, but it will have limited appeal and you may have to wait a long time for the right buyer. A popular boat from a known builder or designer or a boat raced extensively in your area will mean a faster sale. Even a sailboat with high potential resale value is rarely a good financial investment. Since you generally can't expect to earn a return on your principal or even break even, the major resale issues are quickness of the sale and the level of depreciation you should expect.

PUTTING IT ALL TOGETHER

Now that you have collected masses of data, you can make a decision in which you will feel confident. Or, you can throw up your hands and flip a coin. Since you have done so much analysis and have carefully narrowed the choices, none of your alternatives can be too bad. If necessary, you can always revalue, rescore, and rerank the boats in your final list, adding price as another criterion. At this stage, also let your aesthetic and emotional biases and preferences play a major role in the decision.

Select the right boat for you, but wait, **don't** tell the dealer or owner about your decision until you have read the next chapter.

XV.

FINALIZING THE SALE

NEGOTIATING

To negotiate the best deal, be prepared to be hard-nosed. Dealers and brokers are professional salespersons, and if they are good, they will be experts in sales techniques. They want to convince you to buy, and they want to obtain the highest possible profit margin. Even the private seller of a used boat will want to get the highest price possible. Your objective, of course, is to get the lowest price, either so you can afford the boat or so you will have money left over to buy equipment or to finance your sailing trips.

The most important rule to keep in mind as you negotiate is that you must resist being prematurely pressured into a final contract. This can be very difficult as you envision yourself at the helm on a sparkling, breezy day. If you demonstrate a thoughtful and methodical approach to your purchase, the seller will be forced to deal with you on your terms. A reasonable delay to obtain more information, ponder your decision, or further negotiate the price will generally result in a better decision and better terms. On those rare occasions when a deal does fall through, remember that your second choice boat probably represents a much better selection than the average boat buyer makes. There are also many other "perfect boats" available that haven't shown up in your decision process. If you lose one boat, take heart, reevaluate, rescore, and start negotiating on another.

One approach to negotiating is to create price competition among the sellers of your top-ranked boats once you have developed their comparable prices. This approach permits you to use a boat with a low cost per pound as leverage to negotiate the price of another boat downward. If you have a strong favorite among the boats under consideration, don't tell that seller. The seller must be convinced that price is so important to your decision that s/he will have to offer the lowest price to make a sale.

Dealer profit margins on new sailboats typically run from 15 to 20 percent. On extra equipment, they may go as high as 50 percent. Use this information to your advantage when making your first offer. For example, your initial offer might be 80 percent of the boat's base price, plus 60 percent of the price of extra equipment, less any credits for unwanted equipment. A first offer on a used boat can be based on either a review of advertised prices for similar boats, with an adjustment for age, condition, and equipment, or on a published guide such as the *BUC Used Boat Price Guide.*

Your first offer on a new or used boat should be low but not unreasonable. If it is too low, you won't be taken seriously. If it is too high, you will have given away part of your bargaining position before you even get started. When the economy is depressed, it is a buyer's market and you can generally get a better price. In any type of economy, you may be able to buy for less than the boat's fair market value if a seller needs cash or a quick sale.

If you are going to finance your purchase, you may want to consider having the seller make all the desired modifications and equipment additions so that you can include those costs as part of the price to be financed. This allows you to distribute your outfitting costs over the length of the loan and gives you use of the equipment and modifications from day one. Although your financing costs will be greater, you may realize corresponding tax benefits.

If you don't want to finance new equipment with the boat, you can still realize savings of 20 to 30 percent by purchasing equipment via discount catalog or through a new boat account with a chandlery. Any equipment installations you do yourself will add further savings.

When you have negotiated a final price with the seller, it should be documented in a sales contract. The contract should include agreed prices for all labor for commissioning, installation of extra equipment, and repairs, as well as prices for all materials and equipment. It should specify warranties offered, list any special terms and contingencies, and identify any other costs—including taxes, cradles, shipping insurance, and yard charges. If the boat is used, you should request written documentation (and a promise of indemnity) regarding removal of prior liens before the sale agreement is finalized. If the boat has a doubtful past with many prior owners, you or your financing institution may want to do your own research to assure that you will receive clear title when you take possession.

FINANCING

There are three customary ways to pay for a boat: cash already in hand; owner- or seller-held contract; and loan from a financial institution. You might work out a plan to combine two or even all of these. Consider all available options. Seller-held contracts can take any form, although your goal will usually be to obtain the longest repayment term and lowest interest rate. Be wary of balloon payments, unless you are certain they can be met or you can refinance. When you shop around for a standard marine loan, check with a large number of banks, savings and loans, and credit unions since loan offerings vary widely. Many institutions are more willing to finance a sailboat documented by the United States Coast Guard.

In deciding among specific seller-held contracts and conventional loans, compare length of time for repayment, down payment required, any limit on amount to be financed or type of boat or equipment that may be financed, level of monthly payments, interest rate and whether it is fixed or will vary, total amount of interest to be paid and any resulting tax benefits, any special fees, whether balloon payments are required, total cost of the boat over the entire period of the financing arrangement, and options in the event of default. Have your attorney review any financial agreement, including seller-held contracts, before you sign.

SURVEYS

Most used boats of wood, metal, and ferrocement should have a full marine survey before you agree to purchase. In fact, most lenders require a survey on a used boat before they will make a loan, and most marine insurance companies require a survey before they will insure an older boat. The survey is expensive because it includes the surveyor's fee, the cost of haul-out, and the cost of any repairs for damage (such as bored holes or pulled fittings) to the boat during the survey. If you have done your homework, the survey will confirm your choice with further technical information concerning the boat's condition. The sale should **always** be contingent upon your satisfaction with the results of the survey.

You can select a surveyor by writing to: National Association of Marine Surveyors, Inc., 305 Springhouse Lane, Moorestown, NJ 08057, Telephone (800) 822-NAMS. You can also get recommendations on a surveyor from a yacht broker, local boatyard, or bank or insurance company marine department. Avoid recommendations from anyone directly involved in selling or financing the boat. Contact the recommended surveyors and ask what type of surveys they do. Most good surveyors specialize, for example, wood boats only, no ferrocement, engines but not rigging. Request the names of owners of boats surveyed previously. Check with these owners to see how close their survey findings were to the realities of owning the boat.

I believe a survey can best meet your needs if you pay the surveyor by the hour. This is a nonstandard approach that makes the survey more expensive, but the findings will be more thorough and should more than pay for themselves in negotiating price and in forecasting maintenance and equipment upgrades. Have as much of the survey done as possible before you make an offer. Haul-out and sea trials will generally be excluded, but the majority of the boat can usually be examined. This can help you decide whether you want to make an offer and the level of your initial offer. Look over the surveyor's shoulder and ask lots of questions. This may drive him/her crazy, but you'll have a better idea of what you're getting into, how serious the problems are, what the options are for fixes, costs, and so forth. Remember YOU'RE buying the boat; the surveyor isn't. Finally, inventory the equipment, list the boat specs, and turn on all the easy and obvious equipment yourself. This will save the surveyor's time for the areas where you need his/her expertise.

In addition to a general survey, it is often a good idea to survey the sails, engine, rigging, and electronics separately. Many surveyors are not sufficiently trained to provide a good assessment on these technical items or systems, which represent a major part of your sailboat investment and have a high potential for problems.

If a large *sail inventory* is included, or if you are doubtful about the sails' condition, take them to a reputable local sailmaker and have them evaluated. The cost is nominal if compared with the thousands of dollars represented by a large inventory. If you have to repair or replace any sails, the boat's price should be discounted accordingly. If you actually finalize the sale, the sails can be left at the loft for any necessary repairs and recutting.

Engines, even on new boats, should be surveyed by a mechanic who regularly services that type of engine. This is important because sailboat engine installations are often inadequate and the engines poorly maintained. If you buy the boat, you will have a list of all the repairs and improvements necessary for a safe and dependable engine. You will save many dollars and much grief if you correct these problems immediately. If your boat is new, the warranty might pay for much of this initial engine work. If the boat is used, the seller should provide additional discounts that should cover all or at least most of the costs of repairs and upgrading.

Rigging—both standing and running—is another system for which a specialist surveyor may be necessary, particularly on a larger boat. If neither your general surveyor nor you feels comfortable in this potentially complex and expensive area, get some assistance, especially if the boat appears to be underrigged, poorly maintained, or has been or will be sailed hard.

Finally, if the boat has a great deal of *electronic equipment,* it will be worthwhile to have it evaluated by a qualified electronics technician. Again, a sizable electronics inventory can represent a large portion of the boat's value, assuming it isn't obsolete or hasn't been severely damaged by salt, moisture, or misuse.

FINAL PRICE ADJUSTMENTS

When all your surveys and evaluations have been finished, you should have extensive information on the boat's condition. If you find that your original judgment about the boat was erroneous, you may want to look for another boat. If the problems identified are minor, correctible, or ones you can live with, you will be a fully informed purchaser. Your list of problems should also be useful in any further bargaining with the seller that you may wish to do. Since you should have insisted that the sale be contingent upon the survey findings, you have a right to ask for modifications in the price based on the cost of correcting the deficiencies identified in a complete survey. When you propose price adjustments, base them on commercial retail rates. Don't assume that you will donate your labor unless you assign no value to your time. Keep in mind while bargaining that some wear and tear is to be expected even on the best maintained used boat and that the seller may have already discounted the price if the boat is less than perfect in one or more areas.

XVI.

OTHER ASPECTS OF THE DECISION

Before you completely relax with your developing expertise on boat buying, there are some other aspects of the decision that you should be thinking about before you take delivery, and perhaps before you even sign a sales contract.

MOORAGE

Where are you going to keep your boat? Will its location be a convenience or a hassle? Serious moorage problems can spoil sailing as easily as a balky engine. As you evaluate moorage, consider a number of questions. What is the annual cost of the berth or mooring? What are future rate increases likely to be? Are electricity, water, and parking available? Is the moorage secure from vandalism and theft? Is it secure from wind and wave damage? What is the exposure to storm conditions, and what is the length of the fetch between the moorage and the windward shore? Will motor-boat wakes cause any problems?

Are there any extreme or unusual electrolysis problems at

the moorage from other boats, leaking shore power, or another source? Is the moorage in fresh or salt water? Electrolysis and corrosion of above and below water metals (particularly electrical equipment) are much less of a problem in fresh water. Although wooden hulls moored in fresh water have no problems with worms, rot is likely to be more of a problem than in salt water.

Will ice affect moorage use during the winter? If you have to row out to the mooring, is there a nearby dock that can be used for loading for long trips or for dockside maintenance?

INSURANCE

Typically, boat insurance will cost 0.7 to 1.5 percent of the value of the boat and its contents. It will be written to cover a specific geographic area, usually the local cruising area. Coverage for sailing beyond the policy's geographic limits can be arranged by amending the policy to cover specific trips. Small boats can be carried on a household insurance policy, but larger ones, including all those that are not easily trailerable, require a more comprehensive marine policy. Since boat prices have been inflating rapidly in recent years, a "replacement value" policy is a good idea. It will provide coverage at current prices for repairs and equipment—less the deductible—up to the policy's value. Of course, you will need detailed records and receipts for all the equipment and improvements to the boat so that the true value of your boat can be substantiated for a claim.

Because of the high cost of offshore coverage, many sailors forgo hull insurance and sometimes even liability insurance. With the money saved, they buy a bigger anchor, more chain, a better life raft, and the like—in effect buying a form of self-insurance. However, in survival conditions, such as the Cabo San Lucas disaster where dozens of boats were lost, even the best preparation may be inadequate. A high deductible, cata-strophic policy will give you the option of starting again with another boat if you ever face a devastating, total loss.

MAINTENANCE

Sailboat maintenance is both time-consuming and expensive. My own rule of thumb is that one day of work is required for each day of sailing. Paying for maintenance is one solution, but it can be very costly. Diesel mechanics are paid up to $45 or more an hour, and boatyard labor costs up to $35 or more an hour. Even if you hire someone, you have to plan the extent of the work and oversee its quality, since one disconnected hose or missing cotter pin could cause a disaster. You still end up doing a great deal of the work yourself, although this does have the advantage of making you and your boat more self-sufficient, a cardinal requirement for serious cruising or racing. You will find that your maintenance skills will grow to accommodate longer and more challenging sailing to ever more remote places.

There are some ways to keep your maintenance to a minimum and your sailing to a maximum. Don't buy a boat— charter or go with a friend. Select the simplest and smallest boat that will meet your requirements. Keep a work list and maintain your boat all year long. Don't get behind and let the work accumulate. When you have work done at the yard or by a professional, ask if you can work alongside. You will save some labor costs, as well as learn new skills. Work on functional items first and cosmetic items second. Invite all the friends and relatives who sailed with you during the year to a work party.

THE FINALE

Make the best decision possible, pay your money, take delivery, and go sailing—enjoy the rewards of your hard work.

CHAPTER

XVII.

HOW TO SELL YOUR BOAT

Before you can buy a new or used sailboat, you may have to sell your old one. The sailboat market has been depressed since the early 1980's and even though the market may come back, selling your boat is still a difficult and emotionally draining experience. In preparation for teaching a course on "How to Sell Your Boat," I learned a lot, particularly from the broker interviews. The following may help you finish one dream so that you can start another.

PREPARING TO SELL

The first thing you should do, whether you intend to sell privately or through a broker, is to strip the boat of excess gear. This means junk, unrepairable equipment, food, half-full cans of teak oil, and so forth. There is nothing more disgusting for a buyer than to open the icebox and find part of a peanut butter sandwich that looks like it grew on Venus. You're incredulous? I see this frequently when helping buyers look at used boats.

Also remove all your personal gear, such as harness, lifejacket, foul-weather gear, and bedding.

Then remove anything that you can use on your next sailboat, unless it is a) Coast Guard required; b) part of the boat's basic inventory of equipment (for example, working sails, at least four bumpers, one working anchor); or c) something that damages the boat or leaves a void when removed ("What used to be here? Oh nothing important, just the engine"). For example, your stern anchor might make a great working anchor on a smaller boat or your storm anchor might become a working anchor on a larger boat. Remember that buying new equipment for your next boat will be costly (have you recently priced the anchor and rode you bought ten years ago?), as well as time consuming. Don't strip your boat too far or it may look underequipped. If equipment is old and worn, obsolete by today's standards, difficult to maintain, or not as effective as you would like, review its replacement cost in dollars and time. In some cases, it may be better to buy new for your next boat.

The reason for stripping the boat of equipment you can use is that only the astute buyers will appreciate extra equipment and they are definitely not the majority. Even informed buyers won't give you fair value for the extra gear, since the marketplace puts a low value on it and they will usually have different ideas on equipping the boat than you. The extra gear will make the boat more marketable, but you will only get about five to ten cents on the dollar for it.

Do any maintenance or repairs that are inexpensive and would be obvious to a potential buyer, for example, the engine won't start; the mainsail is ripped in half; wiring is hanging loose all through the cabin; or the boat rapidly takes on water after being launched. DON'T spend a lot of money upgrading the boat, since you will only get back a small percentage of your investment, if that. For instance, a complete new paint job is rarely cost effective on a large boat, but on a small boat repainting with a simple one-part marine enamel can have an enormous payoff, since the cost of materials is low and the time investment small. I once did minor patching on two kayaks, repainted them, added air bags, and then sold them for 225 percent of their purchase price.

CLEAN, CLEAN, CLEAN. Whether you sell privately or through a broker, you will either have to do this yourself or pay a detailer to do it. Payback here is very high, adding perhaps 10 percent or more to the final sale price and making the boat much more marketable. It makes a very good first impression and will help your boat to stand out from the masses of filthy boats that are on the market. A clean boat is also considered a good indicator of the overall mechanical condition of the boat.

PRICING YOUR BOAT

If you decide to sell the boat yourself, rather than through a broker, your first task is to set a price. Unfortunately, you probably have an unrealistic idea of what your boat is worth. Typically, a) you're emotionally involved with the boat; b) when you bought, the dealer told you that it was an investment like a house that would appreciate and the inflation of the 70's and early 80's supported that illusion; and c) you don't have a realistic view of the market. To realistically price your boat, review the ads and listings for sisterships or comparables. From these reviews, calculate an average asking price, plus a high and a low price. Then add or subtract to your boat's target price, based on its equipment; any special features; repairs needed; its age; whether there is an active class association or fleet; whether the builder is still in business; the overall quality of the boat when it was constructed; the reputation of the designer; trends in design; and its overall condition and cleanliness. You might also look up your boat in a boat "blue book," such as the *BUC Used Boat Price Guide*. These guides purport to show actual sale prices, getting prices, not asking. Now take your revised target price and adjust for local market conditions, popularity of this boat in your area, and your need to sell. Does this sound complicated? It is. Another approach is to hire a surveyor or appraiser to price the boat for you.

Remember when pricing the boat that you have a large "opportunity cost" every day that you don't sell it. Your indirect costs are the interest you are losing on the capital tied up in your boat and the time involved in selling the boat. To this add the direct costs of insurance, moorage, annual maintenance, haul-out, and advertising. On a $100,000 boat, direct and indirect costs could easily amount to over $14,000 by the end of a year. And this doesn't include the emotional stress of showing the boat, bargaining, and deferring the purchase of your next dream boat. Selling now for less may actually net you more dollars and peace of mind.

MARKETING YOUR BOAT

For small boats, I would suggest using bulletin boards, club newsletters, word of mouth, and neighborhood advertising flyers. Larger boats can justify a substantial budget for advertising. Good bets are usually your Sunday newspaper classified section and any local boating magazines. Large or unique boats are worth advertising in national boating magazines or listing services, since these are the type of boats that buyers will typically shop for through regional or national searches. A "For Sale" sign on the boat never hurts, particularly if the boat has any visibility.

Be available to answer your phone. Every call you miss may be a lost sale. **SHOW THE BOAT.** You must adapt your schedule to the buyer. This means staying home evenings and all weekend when you place an ad. (See how much fun this is!) Be prepared for a large number of "no-shows." Make sure that buyers can find your boat by preparing a map to the boat that you can send prospective buyers and post in your moorage area.

Putting together a brochure on your boat is a must. List the boat's designer, builder, basic specifications and dimensions, engine, rigging, sails, interior layout, and all equipment (by category) that is included with the boat. List each piece of equipment separately within each category. For example, don't say "three winch handles"; instead list as "one 8-inch non-locking single handle, two 10-inch locking double handles." Include color photographs and drawings of the boat in your brochure.

SHOWING THE BOAT

Before a prospective buyer arrives at the boat, wash the decks down and open the boat to air. If it's winter, turn the heater up. Straighten the boat up as if you were going to have company. Wipe up any obvious water or condensation and pump the bilge. When the prospects arrive, give them a copy of your brochure and make your log and maintenance records available for their inspection. You do have all your maintenance records, right? Offer them a hot or cold drink as appropriate.

DON'T TALK TOO MUCH. Let the prospective buyers sell themselves. Answer questions succinctly. When you see a glazed look in their eyes, quit talking. Be prepared to answer the question "Why are you selling?" Remember this rule of the brokers and you will avoid taking a lot of unproductive "joy sails": **NO SEA TRIALS WITHOUT A DEPOSIT.**

THE SALE

Be prepared to bargain. Most buyers expect to make a lower offer and then receive a counteroffer. When you reach agreement, ask for a deposit of from 5 to 20 percent to hold the boat for one to two weeks for sea trials and survey. Have your attorney draw up a sales agreement that describes the boat and the terms of the sale, including the deposit/earnest money. All parties should sign and retain copies.

A sale is usually contingent upon satisfactory sea trials and a survey, but this is the buyer's worry, not yours. Your only concern is that it take place in a reasonable time period so that the sale can be completed. All costs and damages associated with the sea trials and/or survey should be borne by the buyer. Normal wear and tear is not a reason for altering the price or letting the buyer out of the sale. Your sales agreement should state all these points. Repairs recommended by the surveyor and problems that become apparent during sea trials generally reopen the price negotiation and may even be cause for the buyer to terminate the agreement if the sales agreement so states. If the buyer tries to back out of the sale without good cause, your agreement should provide that you have the option of keeping the earnest money as damages for taking the boat off the market. I would generally recommend keeping a lesser amount, however, that approximates your direct loss from removing the boat from the market. Remember, you want to sell your boat, not get into a feud with a potential buyer.

When you close the sale, accept ONLY a money order or a cashier's check. Notify the state titling agency, the Coast Guard (if the vessel is documented), and your insurance agent of the sale. Make sure you keep copies of all documents associated with the sale, so you can prove you are no longer the owner of the vessel when the Coast Guard calls about seeing your boat offloading bales (of hay?) at midnight.

Here are some unique ways to market your boat for a private sale, although they could also be used with a brokerage sale if your broker approves:

- Offer X hours of free consultation on how everything on the boat works.
- Offer X hours of free maintenance.

- Offer X number of free sailing lessons.
- Offer to pay for sailing lessons at a certified school.
- Offer a guarantee on part or all of the boat for X period. Make sure that any guarantee you offer is conditional and doesn't place you at risk of unlimited liability or cost.
- Use a GOOD photo of the boat in your advertising. Use a color photo if possible.
- Write up a short synopsis of the boat's history, particularly if it is unusual in any way.
- Make a video of the boat.
- Offer a finder's fee.

THE BROKERAGE SALE

If you are discouraged about trying to sell your boat yourself, you should consider selling through a broker. Some boats are better sold privately, and a few boats are almost always better sold through a brokerage. Others can be sold either way.

Boats twenty feet and under should generally be sold privately. They are much more marketable because of their low price, and most brokers aren't interested in them because they bring a low commission. I was told frequently during interviews of brokers that it was almost as much (and sometimes more) work to sell a small boat as a large boat. I believe them. Boats between twenty to twenty-seven feet are in a gray area, since a private sale is feasible, but more brokers will handle them. Even if a broker agrees to sell a boat in this range, you may find that it won't get the attention that the larger boats will. Unless they are specialists in small boats, I find that most brokers prefer to handle boats that are no smaller than twenty-six to thirty feet. Large boats get the best attention at most brokerages and benefit from the extra promotion that results if the listings are shared among different brokerages.

If you have a boat that is in the size range where you have a choice on a private versus brokerage sale, ask yourself two questions. First, how marketable is your boat? This may be difficult for you to ascertain objectively without outside assistance. If the boat is a type that is very popular or is so special that it will be easy to sell, a private sale is much easier. Second, are you willing to invest the time and money to have a successful outcome? The private sale should be treated as a serious business. Without that commitment, selling your own boat could be a long drawn-out disaster unless you are very lucky. Brokers who work hard and get a good price within a reasonable time earn every dollar of their commission.

If you decide to let a broker handle your sale, do a little research before you sign a listing agreement. Large brokerages often have better customer traffic and can provide excellent service, including enough sales staff to cover the boats throughout the week. On the other hand, if your boat is average, it may get lost in the crowd. If it is in below average condition, it may look sick next to the other boats. If the brokerage also sells new boats, they may have a vested interest in pushing them, since the profit is substantially more than the typical brokerage commission on a used boat.

A small brokerage may provide more personal service and keep your boat from blending into the dock. Small brokerages may not, however, always have someone on the dock to handle customers, as I discovered when doing broker interviews. This could mean a lost sale on your boat.

Whatever size brokerage you eventually decide to use, it is better for your boat to be shown with similar boats by a broker who has experience with your type. For example, your classic old woody won't get too much buying interest at a brokerage that sells 98 percent fiberglass.

Before making your final selection of a broker, ask for the

names of at least two current listings and two listings that were sold. Call these clients of the broker and ask some hard questions about how satisfied they are or were with the broker's services.

Prepare to sell the boat just as you would if you were selling privately. Remove any equipment you want to keep, make any obviously needed repairs, and clean the boat. The broker won't do this for you and failing to do so will definitely cost you bucks. Now take the boat to the broker.

When you use a broker, you can expect to pay a 10 percent commission, plus a moorage fee if the boat is shown at the broker's docks. If the boat needs minor repairs, painting, or cleaning that you failed to do, the broker will usually recommend that you do this yourself or will help make arrangements with a detailer. All costs of detailing and repairs to help sell the boat are paid by you as seller. Normal advertising and promotion is included in your contract with the broker, but occasionally you may be asked to pay part or all of special promotions for your boat.

During the time the boat is displayed by the broker, you are expected to perform normal maintenance and cleaning and to keep up your marine insurance policy. I frequently see boats in brokerages that look semiabandoned because they haven't been visited by their owners in months. This is obvious to prospective buyers, who will usually gravitate toward a boat that looks more cared for. Check out and clean your boat weekly if you want it to look in top shape.

Brokers will help you set a price on your boat, based on your sense of its value, their experience, the overall condition of the boat (usually based on a thirty- to sixty-minute quick evaluation), and the use of listing or computer services. A percentage may be added to provide bargaining leeway. In a depressed sailboat market, I would be hesitant to add much of a "pad" for bargaining, unless the boat is a very special case. If a quick sale is required, I would even suggest discounting the price 10 to 20 percent, if you have any evidence that it will facilitate the sale. Most brokers do not recommend setting a price range, since the price automatically falls to the lower end of the range.

You should expect the broker to distribute your listing to listing services and to a large number of other brokers at least monthly, and you should see your boat listed in the broker's regular ads. Brokers who don't share their listings with other brokers or advertise intensely are a poor bet for selling your boat. Make sure your boat is in a slip or lot location that has good traffic flow and visibility. Check to see how good your boat looks from the normal direction of the traffic flow.

Don't expect to be involved in showing the boat or negotiating. This is what you are paying the broker for. Brokers generally feel that, with some exceptions, having the seller involved any time prior to closing makes the sale much more difficult. This opinion of the typical sailor's sales ability may make you reconsider your plan to sell privately.

The broker should financially "qualify" and screen potential buyers for you, so that only serious offers with a deposit are sent to you. **ALL** real offers, no matter how low, should be forwarded to you, so you can rethink your price position and perhaps counteroffer. Many initial offers are "lowball" just for bargaining purposes, and the buyer may in fact pay a higher price if you're willing to negotiate. Trades for real estate, autos, airplanes, boats, and so forth are often offered, but brokers say these deals are rarely closed.

Constantly reevaluate your broker's performance. The typical listing agreement is for ninety days and the end of that period would be a good time to do your first assessment of how well the broker is doing for you. If your boat hasn't sold for an extended period, it should be repriced, repaired and/or detailed, moved to a better location for showing, or be renamed, repainted, or sunk.

APPENDIX A

SEA TRIALS CHECKLIST

BOAT:_____

1.0 HELM UNDER POWER.

    1.1 Visibility of gauges.
    1.2 Access to engine controls.
    1.3 Use of bilge pump.
    1.4 Comfort.
    1.5 Steering from the rail.
    1.6 Top speed.
    1.7 Cruising speed.
    1.8 Vibration and noise, alignment.
    1.9 Backing downwind.
    1.10 Handling, close quarters.

2.0 HELM UNDER SAIL.

    2.1 Visibility forward, including checking trim of sails.
    2.2 Visibility of instruments.
    2.3 Steering from the rail.
    2.4 Weather helm.
    2.5 Balance.

2.6 Tracking.

2.7 Access to sail controls.

2.8 # of degrees between tacks.

3.0 RUNNING RIGGING.

3.1 Halyards.

3.2 Winches.

3.3 Sheets.

3.4 Traveler.

3.5 Vangs and preventers.

3.6 Main topping lift.

3.7 Furling or roller reefing.

3.8 Reefing, other mainsail controls.

4.0 MAST & RIG TUNE.

5.0 HULL STIFFNESS, OILCANNING.

6.0 MOVEMENT ON DECK.

7.0 MOVEMENT BELOW DECKS.

7.1 Companionway.

7.2 Handholds.

7.3 Head.

8.0 LEAKS.

9.0 TURN ON EVERY INSTRUMENT AND PIECE OF EQUIPMENT. LIST ALL THOSE NOT WORKING.

APPENDIX B

STARTER LIST OF TOOLS AND SPARE PARTS

Tools:

- Crescent wrench
- Set of metric and English box wrenches
- Set of metric and English hollow-key or hex wrenches
- Set of socket wrenches with English and metric sockets: 1/2-inch, 3/8-inch, and 1/4-inch drives and a variety of extensions, adapters, and universal joints
- Pliers: blunt, tapered, and needle-nosed
- Variety of Phillips, Prince Head, and slot screwdrivers
- Visegrips wrench(es)
- Steel and rubber hammers
- Nicopress tools
- C-clamps
- Hand drill and bits
- Bolt cutters, large enough for the heaviest standing rigging on board

- Hacksaw and spare blades
- Set of miniature pliers, screwdrivers, and electrical wrenches
- Basic tap and die set
- Wire cutter/stripping/crimping tool
- Chisel and punch
- Wood and metal files
- Pry and crowbars
- Ax
- Inspection mirror
- Extension fingers to retrieve lost items from the bilge
- Small vise on a 2 × 12 or larger plank
- Knife and fid
- Plumber's basin wrench
- Small brushes

SPARE PARTS:

- Extra engine and transmission oil
- Light and heavy oils (such as LPS 1 and 3), petroleum jelly, rudder and shaft grease
- Spare fuel filters
- Spare oil filters
- Fuel additives
- Spare injectors and glow plugs for a diesel; spark plugs, condenser, points, distributor cap, rotor, and distributor wires for a gas engine
- Spare belts
- Tape and wire

- Electric wire and connectors of assorted sizes
- Spare bulbs, fuses, and dry cells for all equipment
- Spare fasteners, washers, and gaskets of various sizes
- Wire clamps and hose clamps
- Thimbles for wire and rope
- Shackles
- Cotter pins of all sizes
- Regulator
- Spare water impellers for engine water pump
- Spare diaphragms, valves, and gaskets for all other pumps, including the marine head
- Spare water and fuel hose in several sizes, plus hose fittings
- Sail repair kit, including: sail cloth and sail tape, battens, sail palm, waxed and unwaxed thread, assorted needles, hanks, slides, grommets, grommet tool, and fids for braided line
- Emergency or spare radio antenna
- Spare radar reflector
- Backup battery or kerosene running and anchor lights
- Epoxies, glues, gasket compound, sealing compound, and Teflon tape
- Small pieces of lumber, including a 4' × 8' sheet of ¼-inch plywood and sheet metal screws for patching hull
- Bearings, springs, pawls, snap rings, and grease for all winches

APPENDIX C

PERFORMANCE CRITERIA CHECKLIST FOR BUYING A SAILBOAT

MANUFACTURER:
MODEL:
BOAT'S NAME:
TYPE OF SAIL PLAN:
TYPE OF HULL:

Performance Criteria	Specific Performance Data	Weight	Score	Wtd. Score
LOA:				
LOD:				
LWL:				
Hull Speed:				
Beam:				
Beam as % of LOA:				

Performance Criteria	Specific Performance Data	Weight	Score	Wtd. Score

Draft:
    Board Up:

    Board Down:

Windage:
    Est. of surface area one side:

    Height of freeboard at bow:

Weight Aloft:

Weight in the ends:
    Overhangs as % of LOA:

Displacement:

    Live-aboard Displacement:

    Ballast-Displacement Ratio:

    Displacement-Length Ratio:

Range of Positive Stability:

    Capsize Screen:

Sail Area:

Performance Criteria	Specific Performance Data	Weight	Score	Wtd. Score
Sail Area-Displacement Ratio:				
Sail Aspect Ratio:				
Total Weighted Score				

APPENDIX D

SELF-SURVEY CRITERIA CHECKLIST FOR BUYING A SAILBOAT

MANUFACTURER:
MODEL:
BOAT'S NAME:
HULL NO.:

Specific Survey Criteria	Specific Survey Data	Weight	Score	Wtd. Score

Specific Survey Criteria	Specific Survey Data	Weight	Score	Wtd. Score

TOTAL WEIGHTED SCORE:

APPENDIX E

SUMMARY DATA FORMAT FOR BUYING A SAILBOAT

MANUFACTURER:
MODEL:
BOAT'S NAME:

A. DESIGNER
Name:
Address:

Telephone:
Background/Reputation:

B. BUILDER
Name:
Address:

Telephone:
Background/Reputation:

C. DEALER/BROKER
Name:
Address:

Telephone:
Background/Reputation:

D. SUMMARY OF MAJOR COMMENTS OF THIRD-PARTY
   EVALUATORS

E. SUMMARY OF TEST SAIL RESULTS

F. SUMMARY OF OWNER REFERENCES
   1. Owner 1:

   2. Owner 2:

   3. Owner 3:

APPENDIX F

PRICING WORK SHEET

	COSTS (*Plus and Minus in $*)		
Boat #:	*1*	*2*	*3*
Base Price (use sail-away or initial asking price)			
+ Structural Modifications			
+ Additional Equipment			
+ Labor for Installations			
− Credit for Equipment Not Received or Installed			
− Credit for Repairs and Deficiencies			
+ Shipping			
+ Commissioning			

COSTS *(Plus and Minus in $) (Cont.)*			
Boat #:	*1*	*2*	*3*

+ Yard, Storage and/or
   Cradle

+ Taxes and
   Special
   Fees

TOTAL REAL
COST

COST PER
POUND (Real Cost/Displacement)

BUYER'S INITIAL
OFFER

SELLER'S
COUNTEROFFER

BUYER'S
SECOND
OFFER

SELLER'S
SECOND
COUNTEROFFER

FINAL PRICE

COST PER
POUND
   (Final Price/
   Displacement)

APPENDIX G

LONG-TERM COSTS WORK SHEET

MANUFACTURER:
MODEL:
BOAT'S NAME:

	COSTS (in $)		
	First-Year	*Estimated Length of Ownership*	*Period of Loan*
+ Down Payment			

+ Payments
    1. Principal
    2. Interest			

+ Annual Excise Taxes and Registration Fees			
− Income Tax Reduction for Interest Paid			

− Other Tax
    Reductions,
    Savings			

	COSTS (in $)		
	First-Year	*Estimated Length of Ownership*	*Period of Loan*
+ Insurance			
+ Equipment and Modifications			
+ Annual Maintenance			
+ Repairs and Tools			
+ Moorage			
− Charter or Other Income			
TOTAL GROSS COST OF OWNERSHIP			
− Estimated Net Resale or Equity Value after Adjusting for Any Loans			
TOTAL NET COST OF OWNERSHIP			
Est. Number of Sailing Days			

COST PER SAILING DAY
(Net Cost/
Estimated Sailing
Days—
This provides a
comparative cost
for ownership
versus chartering.)

APPENDIX H

SAILBOAT EVALUATION CHECKLIST

BOAT:_____

1.0   SAMPLE QUALITY INDICATORS

    1.1   Quality of fiberglass:
    1.2   Condition of wood, interior and exterior:
    1.3   Finish and cleanliness of bins and lockers:
    1.4   Condition of bilge:
    1.5   Condition of sample winch:
    1.6   Log available for inspection?:

2.0   KEELS AND BALLAST

    2.1   Centerboard or daggerboard
        2.1.1   Trunk:
        2.1.2   Hinge:
        2.1.3   Lifting mechanism:
    2.2   Keel shape:
    2.3   Ballast material:
    2.4   Keel bolts and access:
    2.5   General condition of keel:

3.0 HULL

    3.1 Fairness:
    3.2 Finish:
    3.3 Fiberglass
        3.3.1 Gel coat—print-through, crazing, cracks:
        3.3.2 Delamination, voids, core rot, moisture:
        3.3.3 Blisters:
        3.3.4 Barrier coat:
    3.4 Wood
        3.4.1 Caulking:
        3.4.2 Rot, worms:
        3.4.3 Fasteners:
    3.5 Metal
        3.5.1 Corrosion:
        3.5.2 Welds:
        3.5.3 Barrier coat:
    3.6 Ferrocement:
    3.7 Insulation:
    3.8 Rub rail:
    3.9 Through-hull fittings NOT evaluated in other sections—type, condition, valves:
    3.10 Zincs:

4.0 DECKS

    4.1 Hull deck joint:
    4.2 Fiberglass
        4.2.1 Stiffness:
        4.2.2 Gel coat:
        4.2.3 Nonskid:
        4.2.4 Core and voids:
        4.2.5 Leaks:
    4.3 Wood
        4.3.1 Rot:
        4.3.2 Leaks:
        4.3.3 Fasteners:
        4.3.4 Finishes:

4.4 Metal
    4.4.1 Corrosion:
    4.4.2 Welds:
    4.4.3 Finishes:
4.5 Teak decks:
4.6 Foredeck comments:
4.7 Sidedeck comments:
4.8 Toe rail or bulwarks:
4.9 Lifelines and pulpits:
4.10 Handholds:

5.0 COCKPIT

    5.1 Comfort:
    5.2 Size:
    5.3 Drainage:
    5.4 Companionway
        5.4.1 Sill or bridgedeck:
        5.4.2 Hatchboards:
        5.4.3 Seahood:
    5.5 Lockers
        5.5.1 Fasteners/hasps:
        5.5.2 Scuppers and drains:
        5.5.3 Size:
    5.6 Coaming:
    5.7 Dodger:

6.0 STEERING

    6.1 Visibility forward:
    6.2 Visibility of compass and instruments:
    6.3 Access to engine controls:
    6.4 Using the running rigging from steering station:
    6.5 Type of steering system:
    6.6 Play in system:
    6.7 Binding in system:
    6.8 Stops:
    6.9 Ease of maintenance:

6.10 Tiller
    6.10.1   Finish:
    6.10.2   Rudder head:
6.11 Wheel
    6.11.1   Number of turns lock to lock:
    6.11.2   King pin:
    6.11.3   Size:
6.12 Emergency tiller:
6.13 Cutlass bearing, shaft bearing, rudder tube, rudder bearings, pintles, and gudgeons:
6.14 Rudder type, size, and location:
6.15 Windvane:
6.16 Autopilot:

7.0 STANDING RIGGING

    7.1   Type of sailplan:
    7.2   Rig complexity, # of stays
        7.2.1   Diameter of stays:
        7.2.2   Size of mast:
        7.2.3   Location of chainplates:
    7.3   Keel stepped mast
        7.3.1   Tie rod:
        7.3.2   Step:
        7.3.3   Heel bolted:
        7.3.4   Partners:
        7.3.5   Mast boot:
    7.4   Deck stepped mast
        7.4.1   Step or tabernacle:
        7.4.2   Compression post:
        7.4.3   Deck reinforcement:
    7.5   Mast
        7.5.1   Mast tune:
        7.5.2   Masthead fitting:
        7.5.3   Spreaders and struts:
        7.5.4   Tangs:
        7.5.5   Drain hole:
    7.6   Mainsail boom
        7.6.1   Cockpit clearance:

7.6.2 Gooseneck:

7.6.3 Boom gallows:

7.7 Jib & staysail booms:

7.8 Spar corrosion, cracks, rot, finish:

7.9 Stays

    7.9.1 Terminals:

    7.9.2 Toggles:

    7.9.3 Clevis pins:

    7.9.4 Cotter pins:

    7.9.5 Turnbuckles:

    7.9.6 Backstay adjuster:

    7.9.7 Running backstays:

7.10 Chainplates:

    7.10.1 Stemhead:

7.11 Bowsprit

    7.11.1 Bobstay:

    7.11.2 Dolphin striker:

    7.11.3 Sprit condition—rot, corrosion:

    7.11.4 Bowsprit platform:

    7.11.5 Anchor position:

7.12 Boomkin:

8.0 RUNNING RIGGING

8.1 Halyards & leads:

8.2 Jib and staysail sheet leads:

8.3 Mainsheet and traveler:

8.4 Mainsail reefing:

8.5 Cunningham, outhaul, downhaul, topping lift, vang, preventer:

8.6 Pole, topping lift, downhaul or foreguy:

8.7 Winches and handles:

8.8 Cleats and stoppers:

9.0 SAILS

9.1 Main:

9.2 Jibs and genoas:

9.3 Staysails:
9.4 Spinnakers:
9.5 Storm sails:
9.6 Other sails:

10.0 ENGINE

10.1 Type (manufacturer, cylinders, horsepower):
10.2 Horsepower to displacement ratio:
10.3 Outboards
    10.3.1 Shaft length, gearing, prop:
    10.3.2 Weight:
    10.3.3 Motor mount or well:
    10.3.4 Controls and alternator:
    10.3.5 Corrosion:
    10.3.6 Alcohol-resistant hoses, gaskets, and fuel pump:
10.4 Fuel tank storage:
10.5 Inboard General
    10.5.1 Location and general access:
    10.5.2 Removal:
    10.5.3 Access
        1) Belts, changing:
        2) Compression release:
        3) Engine and heat exchanger zincs:
        4) Engine to shaft alignment:
        5) Exhaust antisiphon valve:
        6) Freshwater drain:
        7) Freshwater fill:
        8) Freshwater pump:
        9) Fuel bleed screw:
        10) Fuel filters:
        11) Fuel pump:
        12) Fuel shutoffs:
        13) Head bolts, torquing:
        14) Injectors:
        15) Ignition system for gas engine:
        16) Oil, engine, dipstick:
        17) Oil, engine, fill:
        18) Oil, engine, drain:

19) Oil, engine, filter:

20) Oil, transmission, fill:

21) Oil, transmission, drain

22) Oil, transmission, dipstick:

23) Seawater drain:

24) Seawater pump:

25) Seawater seacock:

26) Seawater strainer:

27) Starter handle:

28) Stuffing box:

29) Valves, adjustment:

10.5.4   Belts, condition:

10.5.5   Cooling System Type:

1) Grate and/or seawater filter:

2) Seacock or ball valve:

3) Condition of hoses, hose clamps:

4) Freshwater, flush T fitting:

10.5.6   Drip pan:

10.5.7   Engine bed and motor mounts:

10.5.8   Engine compartment insulation:

10.5.9   Engine fire extinguisher system:

10.5.10 Exhaust

1) Seacock or ball valve:

2) Antisiphon:

3) Condition:

10.5.11 Fuel Tank

1) # of tanks:

2) Material:

3) Construction (baffles, inspection, secure):

4) Sump:

5) Condition:

6) Fittings:

7) Vent:

8) Fuel fill:

10.5.12 Fuel System

1) Fuel line condition, hose clamps:

2) Fuel cutoffs:

3) Fuel filters:

10.5.13 Gauges
    1) Tach:
    2) Amp and volt:
    3) Oil pressure gauge and alarm:
    4) Cooling temperature and alarm:

10.5.14 Propeller Shaft
    1) Alignment:
    2) Stuffing box:
    3) Cutlass bearing:
    4) Hose sealing cutlass to stern tube:

10.5.15 Propeller
    1) Type:
    2) Location:
    3) Condition:
    4) Brake:

10.5.16 Ventilation:

10.6   Gasoline Inboard Engine
    10.6.1 Ignition system:
    10.6.2 Spark arrester:
    10.6.3 Proper venting:
    10.6.4 Alcohol-resistant hose, gaskets, and fuel pump:

11.0   ELECTRICAL

    11.1   Bonding of engine, shaft, stuffing box, bronze shoe, through-hulls with #8 wire:
    11.2   Lightning ground:
    11.3   Panel
        11.3.1   Location:
        11.3.2   Separate 12 volt and 110 volt:
    11.4   Alternator:
    11.5   Batteries and box:
        11.5.1   Capacity:
    11.6   GFCIs:
    11.7   Lights
        11.7.1   Interior:
        11.7.2   Deck lights/spreader:

11.7.3 Running lights:
11.7.4 Anchor and/or strobe:

12.0 VENTILATION, WINDOWS, HATCHES

12.1 Condition and scuppering:
12.2 Recommended addition of vents and hatches:
12.3 Storm shutters:
12.4 Interior ventilation:

13.0 HEAD

13.1 Type:
13.2 Condition:
13.3 Holding tank system:
13.4 Seacocks:
13.5 Antisiphon:

14.0 WATER SYSTEM

14.1 Tanks
14.1.1 # of tanks:
14.1.2 Material and capacity:
14.1.3 Construction:
14.1.4 Cleanliness:
14.1.5 Vents:
14.1.6 Fills:
14.2 Pumps:
14.3 Sinks
14.3.1 Depth and location:
14.3.2 Sea cocks:

15.0 REFRIGERATOR/ICEBOX

15.1 Type:
15.2 Size:
15.3 Insulation:
15.4 Lids:
15.5 Drain:

16.0 STOVES AND HEATERS

    16.1 Stoves
        16.1.1 Gimbaled, counterweights, lock:
        16.1.2 Sea rails, potholders:
        16.1.3 Crash bar:
        16.1.4 Belt:
        16.1.5 Secured:
    16.2 Heaters
        16.2.1 Crash bars:
        16.2.2 Vented:
    16.3 Installation
        16.3.1 Fuel cutoffs, manual and solenoid, flame out shutdowns:
        16.3.2 Insulation and clearance:
        16.3.3 Stacks and Charley Noble:
        16.3.4 Propane locker:
        16.3.5 Fuel tank or bottles:
        16.3.6 Pressure gauge:
        16.3.7 Fuel lines:
        16.3.8 Bilge blower and propane sniffer:

17.0 INTERIOR

    17.1 Companionway ladder:
    17.2 Handholds:
    17.3 Sole:
    17.4 Wet locker:
    17.5 Storage:
    17.6 Berths:
    17.7 Dinette:
    17.8 Chart table:
    17.9 Fiddles:
    17.10 Heavy weather latches, gear tie downs:
    17.11 Access to hull and deck fittings:
    17.12 Leaks:
    17.13 Bilge:

GLOSSARY

AFT: Toward the stern; the aftermost end of a hull.

ANCHOR SAIL: A small flat sail that is set on the backstay of a sloop or cutter to keep the boat weathervaned into the wind, and hopefully into the waves. Very useful for improving the ride in a nonprotected anchorage.

ANTISIPHON ELBOW: A U-shaped fitting with a minute valve at the top of the U, which is installed in a high loop above the waterline in any hose system (exhaust, bilge pumps, head, etc.) that exits underwater. Prevents backsiphoning of water into the engine, head, bilge, etc., which could cause damage to or sinking of the boat.

AUXILIARY ENGINE: A small engine on a sailboat that is intended for intermittent use, such as anchoring, going in and out of harbors, and making a course in a flat calm. On an auxiliary sailboat the prime means of propulsion is intended to be the sails, *not* the engine.

BABY STAY: The *stay* that runs aloft from a few feet forward of the *mast*. Provides additional forward support for the mast and reduces unwanted backward bending (referred to as "pumping") of the lower portion of the mast.

BACKSTAY: A wire attached to the stern part of the boat and running to the top of the *mast*. Provides support for the mast against the pull of the *forestay* and the *jibs* or *genoas*. See **FORESTAY; SHROUD.**

BACKSTAY ADJUSTER: A mechanical device to easily reduce or increase the tension of the *backstay* for different sailing conditions.

BACKWINDED: The condition of a sail when either the boat's heading or the sail's trim causes the wind to be on the wrong side of the sail. The effect is to slow the boat, cause an accidental jibe, or even sail backwards.

BAFFLE: A partial panel constructed in a water or fuel tank to separate it into two or more sections. This prevents the rapid movement of liquid from one side of the tank to the other. Baffles reduce the internal stress on tanks caused by this movement as the boat heels and pitches.

BAGGYWRINKLE: Recycled rope that is wrapped around *stays*, *spreader* tips, etc., to reduce *chafe* damage to sails.

BALL VALVE: Ball valves are designed for marine and industrial applications. The working part of the valve is a round ball with a hole through the center, which is attached to a handle on the outside of the valve housing. When the handle is parallel to the end openings on the valve, it is in the open position. When the handle is turned 90 degrees from the length of the valve (openings on either end) it is in the closed position.

BAREBOAT CHARTER: The charter of a cruising boat without hired crew members.

BATTENS, FULL: Narrow slats (usually made of wood or fiberglass) that slide into pockets in the *leech* of a mainsail or *jib*. Battens control sail shape and support the extra sail area called the *roach*. A full batten runs from the *leech* to the *luff* of the sail.

BATTERY, MARINE DEEP-CYCLE: A heavily constructed battery with thick plates designed for numerous deep discharges (more than 50 percent of the battery's rated capacity).

BEATING: To sail upwind or as close to the wind as possible via a zigzag course. Also referred to as "going to weather," "closehauled," or "hard on the wind."

BERTH, QUARTER: A berth in the *aft* part of the boat on either side of the *companionway* stairs, often located partially under the *cockpit*.

BLANKET: When one sail blocks the wind of another.

BLOCK: A pulley through which lines are fed and held. A block changes the lead of a line and, in conjunction with other blocks, provides mechanical advantage.

BOBSTAY: A chain, rod, or wire which leads from the end of the *bowsprit* to the bow of the boat at the waterline. It secures the bowsprit and the *mast* by providing downward tension against the upward pull of the *forestay*.

BOLLARD: A vertical T-shaped fitting on a boat to which mooring lines are attached. Serves the same purpose as a cleat or *samson post*.

BOOM: A wooden or aluminum spar which is attached to the *foot* of a sail.

BOOM GALLOWS: A horizontal framework, usually with three slots, on which the *boom* rests when not in use.

BOOM TENT: A cover or awning that goes over the mainsail *boom* to protect the *cockpit* from the sun and rain.

BOOM, WISHBONE: A double elliptical *boom*. The forward edge of a wishbone is set slightly up the *luff* of the sail with the *aft* end attached to the *clew*. The boom curves to each side of the sail with the sail's *foot* kept loose.

BO'SUN'S CHAIR: A seat made from a board, sling, and/or heavily sewn material in which a crew member can be hauled aloft to inspect and repair rigging. (Also spelled "boatswain's," but always pronounced bo'sun's.)

BOWSPRIT: A spar that projects out from the bow of the boat and provides support for longer and additional *forestays*, hence more and larger *foresails*.

BRIDGE DECK: A raised deck immediately *aft* of the main *companionway*, often incorporated into the *cockpit* as a seat. A bridge deck strengthens the construction of the cockpit, increases interior space, and reduces the exposure of the boat to flooding through the companionway.

BROACH: The condition of a boat when it suddenly turns sideways to the wind. This usually happens when sailing downwind with too much sail, in heavy weather, or with a *spinnaker* at its upper wind range. The result is a loss of steerage and a possible capsize.

BTU: British Thermal Unit. A measure of fuel energy.

BULKHEAD: A lateral partition built belowdecks that provides structural support for the boat.

BULWARK: An upward extension of the hull that forms a low wall around the edge of the deck. Keeps the decks drier in moderate conditions and provides additional security for the crew.

CABIN TRUNK: A raised structure over the deck which provides additional headroom belowdecks and a location for the installation of ports and windows.

CAM CLEAT: A small spring-loaded device with two toothed jaws on swivels used for holding lines under load.

CAULKING: Filling in the gaps between planks of a wooden boat. Traditionally was made of oakum and pitch, but is now usually a synthetic compound.

CHAFE: Wear and tear on *running rigging* and sails caused by rubbing against a sharp or hard surface.

CHAINPLATES: Metal fittings attached to the hull, deck and/or *bulkheads*, which secure the *shrouds* and *stays* supporting the *mast*.

CHANDLERY: A sailor's toy store.

CHARLEY NOBLE: The cap on the stack or chimney of a galley stove or cabin heater. Lets the smoke out and keeps the rain and spray from getting in.

CHASE BOAT: A small powerboat used by *bareboat charter* companies to bring emergency parts, supplies, and mechanics to their charter boats for on-site repairs.

CLAM CLEAT: A V-shaped cleat with teeth which grasps a line securely.

CLEVIS PIN: A strong metal pin that fits into and fastens one fitting to another. A clevis pin is usually secured by a cotter pin. Clevis pins are used extensively in the *standing rigging*.

CLEW: The *aft* bottom corner of a sail to which the *sheets* are attached.

COACH ROOF: The top of the *cabin trunk*.

COAMING: A raised lip or short solid rail (wall) constructed around hatches, *companionway* openings, and *cockpits* to stop the flow of water.

COCKPIT: The sunken area on deck where the crew sits. Usually the main cockpit is in the *aft* part of the boat. The main *companionway* going below decks is usually entered from the cockpit.

COMPANIONWAY: The opening with a ladder or stairway that leads from the *cockpit* or deck to the cabin below.

COMPRESSION BAR or **POST:** A wooden post or metal pipe installed from the deck to a reinforced floor, directly underneath a deck-stepped mast. Reinforces the deck and provides support for the compression loads of the *mast.*

CONVECTION HEATER: Provides heat through the natural circulation of air. Draws cool air from below and expels hot air to the ceiling.

CORED FIBERGLASS: A technique used to construct stiff decks and hulls while using less fiberglass. A core of foam, plywood, or balsa is bonded to an inner and outer skin of fiberglass.

CRUISING SPINNAKER: A large light sail of nylon for off-the-wind sailing. In size it falls between a drifter and a full *spinnaker.* A cruising spinnaker is cut in a slightly asymmetrical shape, and fastens to the bow with a *tack pendant* and with one or more hanks to the *jibstay.* It is easier to handle than a full spinnaker. Also referred to as a "gennaker."

CRUISING THROTTLE: The engine speed at which noise, vibration, and fuel economy are acceptable for the crew. Operating above cruising throttle for long periods of time usually results in increased engine wear.

CUNNINGHAM: A line used to adjust the tension on the *luff* of a *mainsail* or *jib.*

DISPLACEMENT: Technically, the amount of water displaced by a boat. Since this amount always equals the boat's weight, the total displacement is often used to measure the boat's size or weight.

DISPLACEMENT SPEED: 1.34 times the square root of the waterline length in feet. Also known as "hull speed."

DODGER COAMING: A short solid rail constructed in front of the *cockpit,* to which the dodger is attached. Also serves as a splash guard, preventing water from running under the dodger.

DOWNHAUL: A line that pulls down on any sail, *spinnaker* pole, *whisker pole,* or *boom.*

DROGUE: A device to slow the drift of a boat or buoy. Usually a conical shape with an opening in the small and large ends like a wind sock.

FAIR: Smooth surface with no bumps, hollows, dimples, waves, lines, or wrinkles.

FENDER BOARD: A wooden board or plank, usually a 2 × 4 or 2 × 6, which is hung outside of the bumpers when moored alongside a dock or pilings with an uneven surface. The board simulates the smooth edge of the dock and keeps the bumpers in their proper position, protecting the hull.

FIBERGLASS TAPING: Long strips of fiberglass cloth that are saturated with resin and then used to affix *bulkheads* and furniture to the hull, deck, and each other.

FIXED WING SAIL: A rigid or semi-rigid sail usually constructed of aluminum, fiberglass, or an exotic material such as Kevlar. A wing sail is very similar to a vertical airplane wing and is usually attached to a rotating mast.

FOIL SECTION: The curved cambered shape of sails and keels on modern sailboats. Resembles an airplane wing.

FOOT: The bottom edge of a sail.

FORE: The front, or toward the bow of a boat.

FORECASTLE: The space at the *fore* of a boat, below the *foredeck*, up to the last compartment toward the bow, which is called the *forepeak*. (**FORECASTLE** is pronounced "fo'csal.")

FOREDECK: The *short deck* at the bow of a boat.

FORESAIL: The *headsail* set closest to the bow. Often used interchangeably with the term *headsail*.

FORESTAY: A wire that provides forward support for the *mast*. A forestay is the farthest *stay* toward the bow, and sails are usually rigged from it.

FORE-TRIANGLE: The area bounded by the *mast*, the deck, and the *forestay*. Its size affects the amount of sail a boat can carry in a jib or genoa.

FREEBOARD: The height of the hull between the boat's waterline and its deck. Also refers to the unimmersed portion of the hull.

FULL HOIST: When a sail is hoisted to its maximum *luff* tension. Also refers to a sail where the *luff* is at the maximum length that can be used on any particular *stay*.

GAFF-RIGGED: A boat whose sails are four-sided and are hung along their top edge from a gaff (the spar on the top of a sail).

GATE VALVE: A valve with a round handle that screws down to close and up to open. Very similar in design to the typical garden faucet.

GEL COAT: A very thin, smooth resin coating used as the outside layer on fiberglass construction. Used to provide color and a final smooth cosmetic surface. Also serves as a barrier coat to prevent the intrusion of water into the fiberglass laminate.

GENOA: A large *headsail*, often much larger than the *mainsail*, which is set on the *forestay*. A genoa overlaps with the mainsail. May also be thought of as a large *jib*.

GIMBALS: Any support that allows an onboard object such as a compass, table, stove, or lamp to pivot with the heel of the boat and so remain level.

GLOW PLUG: A heating element, very similar in shape to a spark plug, that preheats the cylinder of a diesel engine to allow a fast and easy start.

GRAPNEL: A small four (or more)-pronged anchor used to pick up objects that have dropped to the bottom. May also be used as a lightweight anchor on rocky bottoms.

GROUND FAULT CIRCUIT INTERRUPTER (GFCI): An extremely sensitive circuit breaker that will turn off all electrical current when there is a micro drop in voltage due to a person becoming a negative ground. It will save your life if you mix electricity and water.

GYPSY: A fitting on a *windlass* around which the anchor chain is led. Provides purchase and grips the chain for hauling in or letting out.

HEAD: The toilet and/or the bathroom on a boat. Also a directional term.

HEADSAIL: The sail(s) set in front of the forwardmost *mast* on the boat. Also used interchangeably with the term *foresail.*

HEEL: A term referring to the angle of a sailboat when it leans to one side while sailing.

HELM: The device that controls the rudder. Both a *tiller* and a wheel are known as the helm. May also refer to the immediate area where the tiller and wheel are located.

HIKE OUT: Leaning far out over the side to balance a *heeling* boat. Hiking by the crew allows a boat to be sailed flatter or more level, and thus to sail faster and closer to the wind without being overpowered.

HULL LINER: A fiberglass shell that fits the shape of the hull and is lowered into and bonded to the hull before the deck is put on. The liner may include much or all of the boat's furniture, and as a minimum includes positions for mounting the boat's cabinet work, bunks, etc. The liner provides a clean-looking interior and may also provide additional stiffness to the boat. Sometimes the lower portion of the liner is referred to as a "pan."

HULL SPEED: See **DISPLACEMENT SPEED.**

IMPELLER: The blades on a rotary pump that draw and force the water through the pump.

INJECTOR: The nozzle on a diesel engine that forces a fine spray of fuel into the cylinder.

JIB: The small *headsail* set on a *forestay*. While jibs do not usually have any overlap with the *mainsail*, as *genoas* do, the terms jib and genoa have become almost interchangeable.

JIBSTAY: When a *jib* is set on a *forestay*, this *stay* is often called a jibstay, particularly on small boats. The terms jibstay, forestay, and headstay are often used interchangeably.

JOINER WORK: Interior woodwork of a boat.

KNOCKDOWN: A violent *heel* to an extreme angle due to heavy seas and/or a strong gust of wind.

LATERAL PLANE: Underwater profile of a boat. The amount of lateral plane has a direct effect on the leeway or sideways direction that the boat will make when sailing.

LAZY JACKS: A bridle of small lines leading from the *mast* or *gaff* down to the *boom* on each side of the sail. Lazy jacks hold and stow the sail when it is lowered.

LEEBOARD or **LEECLOTH:** A padded plank or canvas fitted to the inside edge of a bunk and held up vertically or at a sharp angle. Keeps a sleeping crewmember from falling to the cabin *sole* when the bunk is on the boat's high side due to *heel* or rolling.

LEECH: The *aft* edge of a sail.

LEECH LINE: A small line run through the outside edge of a sail's *leech* to control flutter of the *roach* and leech.

LEEWARD: The direction toward which the wind is blowing, or the downwind side of a boat. (Pronounced "loo'ard.") See **WINDWARD.**

LINE STOPPERS: A cam-type cleat with a handle that grips a line. Usually used for *halyards*, *topping lifts*, *downhauls*, *reef lines*, and other *running rigging* where multiple lines are led to a single winch. Line clutches are a more sophisticated type of line stoppers.

LOA: Length overall. The total length of a boat, including all significant overhangs that are a permanent part of the boat, such as bowsprits and boomkins.

LUFF: The forward-facing edge of a sail. Also the flutter that a sail makes when it is improperly trimmed or the boat is headed too close to the wind. A sail usually starts luffing at the luff.

LUGS: The plastic or metal fittings attached to the *luff* or *foot* of a sail, which secure the sail to the *mast* or *boom* by sliding in a groove or on a track.

MAINSAIL SHELF: An additional area of sailcloth with a curved seam, which is constructed in the foot of a mainsail. With the *outhaul* slightly slack, the shelf fills out, giving the mainsail slightly more sail area and a fuller, more powerful shape for lighter winds or off-wind sailing.

MAINSHEET: The line that controls the angle of the *mainsail* to the wind. Typically it is attached toward the *aft* end of the *boom*.

MARCONI RIG: A tall sailing rig with a triangular-shaped mainsail. It is the most typical rig on modern sailboats.

MAST: A vertical spar from which sails, or other spars carrying sails, are hung.

MAST BOOT: A waterproof sleeve that fits around the *mast* where it goes through the deck.

MASTHEAD: The top of the *mast.*

MAST HEEL: The bottom of the *mast.* Also referred to as the "butt."

MAST STEP: The groove or box in which the *mast heel* is set when the *mast* is mounted, or stepped.

MIZZENMAST: The smaller *aft* mast on a yawl or ketch.

MIZZEN STAYSAIL: A light, triangular-shaped *reaching* sail set forward of the *mizzenmast.*

NICOPRESS TOOL: A tool used to squeeze Nicopress fittings onto wire rigging. Nicopress fittings are used to seize eyes and thimbles onto wire or to join two pieces of wire.

OUTHAUL: A line used to pull the *foot* of a sail tightly toward its *clew* in order to flatten it.

PITCH: The seesawing up and down action of the bow and stern in waves.

PITCHPOLE: When a boat buries its bow, and its stern is lifted up over 90 degrees, causing a somersault. This usually happens only when running in large seas.

PLANE: The action of a boat when it moves over, rather than through, the water, due to a combination of speed and hull design.

PLUMBER'S BASIN WRENCH: A plumbing wrench designed to reach up under sinks to tighten the nuts on faucets. Very useful in tight spots.

POCKET CRUISER: A small sailboat designed for cruising versus day sailing or racing. Usually under 24 feet.

POOPED: To be caught from behind by a large wave that fills the *cockpit.*

POT HOLDER: Springs, wires, or brackets designed to hold a pot or pan on a stove despite the boat's motion.

PREVENTER: A line rigged to the outboard side of a *boom* to prevent it from swinging suddenly inboard should the wind shift to the other side of the sail.

REACH: Sailing when the wind blows across the boat from the side. A reach is any point of sail between close-hauled and *running.*

REEFING: A method of reducing sail area as the wind increases, by rolling or folding a sail, usually from its foot.

REEFING TACK HOOKS: Heavy hooks bolted to the *stemhead* or the gooseneck, which fasten down the reef tack points on a sail when it is reefed.

REEF LINES: Lines used to reduce sail area when *reefing.* Typically in slab or jiffy reefing, there is a reefing line for each new *tack* and *clew* as the sail is progressively reefed down.

REEF PENDANTS: The lines that run through the *reef points.*

REEF POINTS: Reinforced grommets in a sail. Short lengths of line are tied through these to gather the loose sail when the sail is reefed.

REGULATOR: Controls the output of the engine generator or alternator and hence the charging of the boat's batteries.

RE-REEVE: To re-lead a line through a *block* or eye.

RIBS: The frames of a boat curving upward and outward from the keel.

RIG TUNING: Setting up the tension on the *standing rigging* so that the *mast* is straight, the rigging and the boat are not stressed or damaged, and the boat will sail at its best.

ROACH: The additional sail area between the *luff* and a straight line drawn through the *head* and *clew* of a sail. Usually held out by battens. The size of the roach is limited by the length of the battens and the position of the *backstay*.

RODE: An anchor line.

ROGUE WAVE: An unusually large wave that is capable of damaging a boat.

ROLLER REEFING: A method of reducing sail area by rolling the *foot* of the sail around a revolving *boom*, or by rolling the *luff* around a wire *stay* or an extrusion set on a stay.

ROLLING: The action of a boat when it rhythmically *heels* from one side to the other.

RUNNING: Following a course before the wind with the sails filled from behind.

RUNNING BACKSTAYS: Wires or lines that run from the *mast* to the stern portion of the deck, and provide extra support to the mast when *running* or *reaching*. When in use the *leeward* one is slack and the *windward* is set up tight. When not in use, they are often taken forward and tied to the *shrouds*.

RUNNING RIGGING: All lines and wires used to control the sails as opposed to those used to hold up the *mast*. *Halyards*, *sheets*, *reef lines*, etc., are all running rigging.

SAFETY HARNESS: A chest harness with a strong rope tether attached to the boat to prevent the wearer from being swept overboard in rough weather.

SAIL-AWAY: The typical MINIMAL outfitting and equipment that is provided for the advertised price of a new sailboat.

SAIL PALM: A partial, reinforced glove used to control needles when repairing sails or heavy canvas.

SAMSON POST: A wooden post mounted on the *foredeck* for securing anchor *rodes* and dock lines to the boat. The traditional samson post went through the deck and was fastened to the structural framework of the boat, including the stem.

SCUPPERS: Drains on deck or in the *cockpit*.

SEA COCK: A valve that is through-bolted to the hull to control the flow of water in through-hull fittings. Constructed similarly to a ball valve, but uses a rotating cylinder.

SEAHOOD: A cover for sliding hatches that helps keep water from coming belowdecks.

SEA RAILS: A low railing around the outside top of a marine stove designed to keep the pots from sliding off.

SEAWAY: A moderate to rough sea in open water.

SELF-BAILING COCKPIT: A watertight, sealed area that has its *sole* above the waterline and will automatically empty of water through drains, *scuppers*, or one-way valves. A self-bailer refers to one of a variety of one-way valves.

SELF-STEERING SYSTEM: A system to keep a boat automatically on course using a wind vane, an auto-pilot, or a system of shock cords and lines run to a boat's *helm* and *sheets*.

SELF-TENDING: No adjustments required. Usually refers to the *helm* or the *sheets*.

SHACKLE: A U-shaped metal fitting with an opening jaw, which is attached to the ends of various *running rigging*. Provides a quick, easy way to attach running rigging to a sail or fitting, or another part of the boat's running rigging or *standing rigging*. A snap shackle serves the same function, but has a quick-release pin.

SHEAVE: A small wheel with a groove on its edge, inside a *block*, through which a line or wire is run.

SHEETS: The lines that control the angle of a sail to the wind. Sheets are attached at the *clew* of a sail.

SHIP'S LOG: The journal of a voyage, including weather, navigation, maintenance, engine, radio, and daily occurrences.

SHOAL DRAFT: A boat with shoal draft draws very little water relative to its size and can therefore sail in shallower waters.

SHROUD: A *stay* running from the side of the boat to the side of the *mast*. Provides lateral support for the mast.

SLAB REEFING: To reef by lowering a sail at its *foot* and securing it to a new *tack* and *clew* that are installed farther up the sail toward the *head*. A sail may have one, two, or three reefs for progressively stronger winds. Also referred to as "jiffy reefing."

SLIDES: See LUGS.

SNATCH BLOCK: A block with a snap *shackle* for fastening it to the deck (may also have a hinged top, so that a line may be dropped into it rather than threaded through it). A snatch block can be moved easily from one location to another—or stolen (snatched).

SOLE: The term used for a floor in a boat, e.g., *cockpit* sole, cabin sole.

SOLENOID: An electrically operated device for opening and closing valves and performing other mechanical functions without the use of an electric motor.

SPINNAKER: A three-sided, symmetrical, lightweight sail set at the bow of a sailboat when the wind is blowing from behind.

SPREADERS: Horizontal struts installed in pairs on each side of the *mast* between the mast and the *shrouds*. Spreaders increase the angle of the shrouds to the mast, creating better lateral support for the mast.

STAY: Any wire or line that supports a *mast*.

STAYSAIL: On a cutter or staysail sloop, the inner or *aft headsail*, which is set inside of the *jib* or yankee.

STEMHEAD: The *chainplate* that fastens the *forestay* to the bow.

STEMHEAD TACK POINTS: The *shackles* or *tack* hooks on the *stemhead*, used for attaching the *tack* of a *jib* or *genoa*.

STORM JIB: A very small, heavily constructed, flat-cut *jib*, for use in heavy weather conditions.

STORM SHUTTER: A strong cover for windows and portholes. Prevents the windows from being stove in during a storm.

STRINGER: A reinforcing or stiffening frame laid *fore* and aft.

TACHOMETER: An instrument to determine engine speed in revolutions per minute.

TACK: The forward lower corner of a sail. Also refers to sailing upwind, and to the action of sailing across the eye of the wind when going from a port to a starboard tack or vice versa.

TACK PENDANT: A short line or wire fastened between the *tack* of a sail and the *stemhead tack points*. A tack pendant raises a sail off the deck.

TERMINAL, WIRE: A fitting with an eye or jaws that is compressed or bonded over the ends of wire rigging. A good wire terminal will have a strength that is very close to that of the wire. *Shackles*, turnbuckles, *toggles*, and other fittings are fastened to the terminal.

THIMBLE: A tear-shaped metal ring with a groove around its edge, around which lines or wire can be spliced or threaded. Thimbles prevent or reduce chafe of line or wire.

TIE-ROD: A threaded rod or wire with a turnbuckle, fastened between the deck (near the mast partners) and the mast belowdecks or the boat's floor. A tie-rod prevents the upward hinging of the deck around a keel-stepped mast.

TILLER: A horizontal fixture, usually made of wood, that is connected directly to the rudder via the rudder stock or shaft. A tiller turns in the opposite direction as the rudder; hence to turn to port, the tiller is put over to starboard, and vice versa.

TOE RAIL: A low rail, only a few inches high, set into the deck to provide better footing, particularly when the boat is *heeled*. Many boats have a toe rail all around the outside edge of the deck.

TOGGLE: A U-shaped fitting that, when installed correctly, permits the fittings above or below the toggle to rotate both athwartships and *fore* and *aft*. Similar to a universal joint.

TOPPING LIFT: A line or wire that holds up a *boom* or pole.

TRANSOM: The flattish surface at the most *aft* part of a boat. Only a "double-ended" boat has no transom at all.

TRAVELER: A track, rod, or line installed athwartships, which allows greater adjustment of the *boom* angle and the *sheet* tension.

TRYSAIL: A small, heavily constructed, flat-cut, triangular sail which is set without using a boom behind the mainmast during very heavy weather.

TURTLE: To "turn turtle" is to capsize so that the boat floats completely upside down.

ULTIMATE STABILITY: The angle of *heel* beyond which a boat will not go except in the most severe and unusual circumstances, such as when hit by a *rogue wave*.

UNSTAYED MAST: A *mast* that is held up without *stays* by its own internal strength and stiffness.

VANE, SELF-STEERING: A small rigid or semi-flexible sail or wing attached by a shaft, gears, or blocks and lines to the boat's rudder or to a separate rudder hung from the self-steering device. By adjusting the angle of the vane to the wind, the auxiliary rudder or the boat's rudder will be turned to keep the boat on course without requiring a helmsperson. Also called "wind vane."

VANG: A system of mechanical purchase (usually hydraulics or a *block* and tackle arrangement) that holds a *boom* down and prevents the sail from twisting off when sailing off the wind.

WEATHER SHIELDS: Canvas cloths fitted to the stern pulpit and/or lifelines to protect the *cockpit* from the wind and seas.

WETTED SURFACE: The surface area, in square feet, of a boat's hull, keel, and fittings, below the waterline.

WHISKER POLE: A pole attached to the *mast* and *clew* of a *jib* or *genoa* that holds the sail out when sailing off the wind. It keeps the sail from collapsing due to wind shifts and inadvertent course changes.

WINDLASS: A hand- or motor-powered winch mounted on the bow that hauls up chain and anchors.

WINDWARD: The direction from which the wind is blowing. Also the upwind side of the boat. See **LEEWARD**.

WORKING ANCHOR: The everyday anchor used for average conditions.

WORKING SAILS: The sails with which a boat is rigged for average conditions. Usually this is the minimum sail inventory of a boat. For example, on a sloop this would be a *main* and *jib*; on a cutter this would be a *main*, *staysail*, and yankee.

YAW: The action of a boat when its bow swings from side to side. A boat that yaws frequently may be referred to as "squirrely."

INDEX

About the Author

Author Chuck Gustafson developed his love for the water before he could walk, spending many of his childhood years on the lakes of Wisconsin. He started sailing M.I.T. dinghies at the University of Wisconsin, and as a Red Cross Water Safety Instructor directed a city swimming program, taught swimming, and baked in the sun as a lifeguard.

In 1981 Chuck started teaching a course on "How to Buy the Best Sailboat" at the University of Washington's Experimental College. His original lecture outline and student handouts became the basis for the first edition of *How to Buy the Best Sailboat*, which is now used as the course text. In the late 1980's Chuck taught a course on "How to Sell Your Boat" at the College, and in 1990 he started a new course, "Cruising Pacific NW Waters." He has lectured and taught on a variety of other topics, including basic sailing, heavy weather sailing, personal clothing and gear, and alternatives to owning a boat. Since 1983 Chuck has instructed and lectured on overboard rescue (Lifesling focus) and since 1984 has presented workshops at the Seattle National Boat Show.

In addition to this book, Chuck has written numerous sailing articles on such topics as buying a sailboat, selling a sailboat, the cruising spinnaker, heavy weather sailing, overboard rescue, transiting Seattle's local locks, boat improvements, and winter sailing. His sailing articles have been published in *Boat Buyer's Guide*, *Dinghy Digest*, *Nor'westing*, *48° North*, *Sailing*, and *Washington* magazines.

When not writing or teaching, Chuck works as a boater's consumer consultant, helping sailors select, purchase, and outfit boats, using the same approach he advocates in his course and in this book. He has evaluated numerous new and used sailboats and to date has been involved in the purchase and outfitting of boats ranging from dinghies to sixty plus-foot custom cutters. Chuck believes consumers should counter the "hard sell" with the "hard buy."

Chuck and his wife, Alice, own a custom Tartan 30 sloop, *Sometimes a Great Notion*, purchased new in 1977 after one and a half years of research. He dreams of a thirty-six-foot LWL, twenty-five thousand-pound displacement, steel-hulled custom cutter with a cold-molded wood deck, but enjoys even more sailing a boat that is paid for. Chuck and Alice cruise extensively in Puget Sound and British Columbia waters.

Chuck founded and was the first chair of the sailing program in The Mountaineers, a twelve thousand-member outdoor club in western Washington. He continues as a member of their Sailing Committee. He is also a member of the Society of Small Craft Designers, Society of Boat and Yacht Designers, the American Boat and Yacht Council, the Sailing Foundation, the Seven Seas Cruising Association, the Northwest Marine Trade Association, and the Speaker's Bureau of the Boat Owners Association of the United States.

In his spare time, Chuck writes about mountaineering, skiing, and travel. He pursues a variety of other sports, including sailboarding, scuba diving, bicycle touring, climbing, hiking, backpacking and cross-country, telemark, and alpine skiing. He teaches nontechnical climbing and cross-country and telemark skiing. Chuck believes every day spent sailing or in the mountains adds a day to your life.